The Best
Stage Scenes
# of 2006

Smith and Kraus Books for Actors
MONOLOGUE AUDITION SERIES
The Best Men's / Women's Stage Monologues of 2005
The Best Men's / Women's Stage Monologues of 2004
The Best Men's / Women's Stage Monologues of 2003
The Best Men's / Women's Stage Monologues of 2002
The Best Men's / Women's Stage Monologues of 2001
The Best Men's / Women's Stage Monologues of 2000
The Best Men's / Women's Stage Monologues of 1999
The Best Men's / Women's Stage Monologues of 1998
The Best Men's / Women's Stage Monologues of 1997
The Best Men's / Women's Stage Monologues of 1996
The Best Men's / Women's Stage Monologues of 1995
One Hundred Men's / Women's Stage Monologues from the 1980s
2 Minutes and Under: Character Monologues for Actors Volumes I and II
Monologues from Contemporary Literature: Volume I
Monologues from Classic Plays 468 BC to 1960 AD
The Ultimate Audition Series Volume I: 222 Monologues, 2 Minutes & Under
The Ultimate Audition Series Volume II: 222 Monologues, 2 Minutes & Under from Literature
The Ultimate Audition Series Volume II: 222 Monologues, 2 Minutes & Under from the Movies
The Ultimate Audition Series Volume II: 222 Comedy Monologues, 2 Minutes & Under

SCENE STUDY SERIES
The Best Stage Scenes of 2004
The Best Stage Scenes of 2003
The Best Stage Scenes of 2002
The Best Stage Scenes of 2001
The Best Stage Scenes of 2000
The Best Stage Scenes of 1999
The Best Stage Scenes of 1998
The Best Stage Scenes of 1997
The Best Stage Scenes of 1996
The Best Stage Scenes of 1995
The Best Stage Scenes for Men from the 1980s
The Best Stage Scenes for Women from the 1980s
The Ultimate Scene Study Series Volume I: 101 Short Scenes for Groups
The Ultimate Scene Study Series Volume II: 102 Short Scenes for Two Actors
The Ultimate Scene Study Series Volume III: 103 Short Scenes for Three Actors
The Ultimate Scene Study Series Volume IV: 104 Short Scenes for Four Actors
Scenes from Classic Plays 468 BC to 1970 AD

If you require prepublication information about upcoming Smith and Kraus books, you may receive our semiannual catalogue, free of charge, by sending your name and address to Smith and Kraus Catalogue, PO Box 127, Lyme, NH 03768. Call us at (888) 282-2881; fax: (603) 643-1831 or visit www.smithandkraus.com.

The Best
Stage Scenes
of 2006

edited by D. L. Lepidus

SCENE STUDY SERIES

A SMITH AND KRAUS BOOK

Published by Smith and Kraus, Inc.
177 Lyme Road, Hanover, NH 03755
www.SmithKraus.com

First Edition: December 2006
10 9 8 7 6 5 4 3 2 1

Cover illustration: *Wardrobe* by Lisa Goldfinger
Cover and text design by Julia Hill Gignoux

The Scene Study Series 1067-3253
ISBN 1-57525-558-8

NOTE: These scenes are intended to be used for audition and class study; permission is not required to use the material for those purposes. However, if there is a paid performance of any of the scenes included in this book, please refer to the Rights and Permissions pages 213–215 to locate the source that can grant permission for public performance.

Contents

Scenes for One Man and One Woman

Scenes for Two Men

Scenes for Two Women

Foreword

The scenes in this book have been culled from the best plays I could find published or produced during the 2005–2006 theater season. Almost all are from published, readily available plays (see the Rights and Permissions section in the back of this book for publication and rights information). A few are from plays that were not published at the time of my selections, though. A good way to find the complete text is via the following Web site: www.findaplay.com; or, ask a helpful person at a theatrical bookstore such as Drama Book Shop (212-944-0595).

Many of my selections are from playwrights of considerable reputation, such as Keith Reddin, Pearl Cleage, and Don Nigro. Others are by future stars such as Ron Fitzgerald, Eisa Davis, Michael Golamco, John Cariani, and Kenny Finkle.

Most of the scenes have characters who are under forty. That's good news for most of the actors who buy this book. Also good news: There are several wonderful *comic* scenes.

In short, this is the best darn scene book I could assemble. I know you will find the perfect piece in it for your audition or class use.

Many thanks to the authors, agents, and publishers who have graciously allowed me to include these wonderful scenes in this book.

D. L. Lepidus

Scenes for
One Man and
One Woman

Almost, Maine
John Cariani

Seriocomic
Man (East) and Woman (Glory): twenty to thirties, but they could be any
   age

This play is about various denizens of a very small town in Maine.
This is the opening scene. It takes place outdoors, under the stars.
The Man has come out of his house in the middle of the night to
find out who this strange woman is who's standing in his yard.

   Note on symbols: The next character to speak should begin his
or her line where the // appears in the speech of the character speak-
ing. The symbol > appears at the end of a line that is not a com-
plete thought. It means that the character speaking should drive
through to the end of the thought, which will be continued in his
or her next lines. Don't stop for the other character's line.

HER HEART

(Music fades. The lights fade up on a woman standing in the front yard
of an old farmhouse in Almost, Maine. She is clutching a brown paper
grocery bag to her chest. She is looking at the sky. A porch light comes on.
We hear a screen door open and slam as a man enters. He watches her
for a while. He is wearing a big warm coat and plaid pajamas.)

MAN: Hello.

WOMAN: *(To him.)* Hello. *(Resumes looking at the stars.)*

MAN: I thought I saw someone . . . I was about to go to bed. I saw you
   from my window . . .

WOMAN: *(Looking at the sky.)*

MAN: Can I — ? . . . Is there something I can do for you?

WOMAN: Oh, no. I'm just here to see the northern lights.

MAN: OK. OK. It's just — it's awful late and you're in my yard . . .

WOMAN: Oh, I hope you don't mind! I'll only be here tonight. I'll see them tonight. The northern lights. And then I'll be gone. I hope you don't mind . . .

MAN: Is that your tent?

WOMAN: Yes.

MAN: You've pitched a tent . . . >

WOMAN: So I have a place to sleep, >

MAN: in my yard . . .

WOMAN: after I see them, I hope you don't mind.

MAN: Well, it's not that I *(mind)* —

WOMAN: Do you mind?

MAN: Well, I don't know if —

WOMAN: Oh, no, I think you mind!

MAN: No, it's not that I mind —

WOMAN: No, you do! You do! Oh, I'm so sorry! I didn't think you would! I didn't think — . You see, it says in your brochure>

MAN: My brochure?

WOMAN: that people from Maine wouldn't mind. *It says (Pulling out a brochure about Maine tourism.)* that people from Maine are different, that they live life "the way life should be," — and that, "in the tradition of their brethren in rural northern climes, like Scandinavia," that they'll let people who are complete strangers like cross-country skiers and bikers and hikers camp out in their yard, if they need to, for nothing, they'll just let you. I'm a hiker. Is it true? >

MAN: Well —

WOMAN: that they'll just let you stay in their yards if you need to? 'Cause I need to. Camp out. 'Cause I'm where I need to be. This is the farthest I've ever traveled — I'm from more towards the middle of the country, never been this far north before, or east, and did you know that Maine is the only state in the country that's attached to only one other state?!?

MAN: Umm . . .

WOMAN: It is! *(Taking in the space.)* Feels like the end of the world, and here I am at the end of the world, and I have nowhere to go, so I was counting on staying here, unless it's not true, I mean, *is* it true? >

MAN: Well —

WOMAN: Would you let a hiker who was where she needed to be just camp out in your yard for free? >

MAN: Well —

WOMAN: I mean, if a person really needed to, >

MAN: Well —

WOMAN: reallyreally needed to?

MAN: Well, if a person really needed to, sure, but —

WOMAN: *(HUGE relief.)* Oh, I'm so glad, then!! Thank you!!

(The woman hugs the man. In the hug, the bag gets squished between their bodies. When they part, the man is holding the woman's bag. The exchange of the bag is almost imperceptible to both the man and the woman, and to the audience. Immediately after hugging the man, the woman resumes looking intently for the northern lights. Then, realizing she doesn't have her bag:)

WOMAN: Oh my gosh! I need that!

MAN: Oh. Here. *(He gives it back.)*

WOMAN: Thank you.

MAN: Sure.

(Beat. She resumes looking at the stars.)

MAN: OK — . OK . . . *(Beat.)* So you're just lookin' for a place to see the northern lights from?

WOMAN: Yeah. Just tonight.

MAN: Well, you know, you might not see 'em tonight, 'cause // you never really know if —

WOMAN: Oh, no. I'll see them. Because I'm in a good place: Your latitude is good. And this is the right time: Solar activity is at an eleven-year peak. Everything's in order. And, boy, you have good sky for it. *(Taking in the sky.)* There's lots of sky here.

MAN: Used to be a potato farm.

WOMAN: I was gonna say — no trees in the way. And it's so flat!?! Makes for a big sky! *(She takes in the sky. Then:)* So — you're a farmer? . . .

MAN: No. *Used* to be a farm. I'm a repairman.

WOMAN: Oh.

MAN: Fix things.

WOMAN: Oh. *(Laughs.)*

MAN: What?

WOMAN: You're not a lobsterman.

MAN: No . . .

WOMAN: *(Explaining.)* I guess I thought that everyone from Maine was a lobsterman and talked in that funny . . . way like they do in Maine, and you don't talk that way . . .

MAN: Yeah, well, I'm from here . . . and this is how we talk up north, pretty much.

WOMAN: Yeah.

MAN: Plus, ocean's a couple hundred miles away. Be an awful long ride to work if I was a lobsterman.

WOMAN: Yeah. Well, anyway, thank you. Thank you for letting me stay. I've had a bad enough time of things lately to be given a bad time, here —

(The man kisses the woman. When they break, the bag has exchanged clutches — he has it. And now we have two stunned people.)

MAN: Oh . . .

WOMAN: *(Frightened, trying to figure out what has happened.)* Um.

MAN: Oh

WOMAN: Um.

MAN: Oh, boy.

WOMAN: Um.

MAN: I'm sorry. I just — . . . I think I love you.

WOMAN: Really.

MAN: Yeah. I saw you from my window and . . . I love you.

WOMAN: Well . . . — that's very nice but there's something I think you should know: I'm not here for that.

MAN: Oh! No, I didn't think you were.

WOMAN: I'm here to pay my respects. To my *husband.*

MAN: Oh —

WOMAN: Yeah: My *husband.* Wes. I just wanted to say good-bye to him, 'cause he died recently. On Tuesday, actually. And, see, the northern lights — did you know this? — the northern lights are really the torches that the recently departed carry with them so they can find their way to heaven, and, see, it takes three days for a soul to make its way home, to heaven, and this is Friday! This is the third day, so, you see, I *will* see them, the northern lights, because they're *him:* he'll be carrying one of the torches. And, see, I didn't leave things well with him, so I was just hoping I could come here and say good-bye to him and not be bothered, but what you did there just a second ago, that bothered me, I think, and I'm not here for that, so maybe I should go // and find another yard —

MAN: No! No! I'm sorry if I've behaved in a way that I shouldn't have, >

WOMAN: No, I think —

MAN: No! I really don't know what happened, >

WOMAN: Well, *I* do, I know what happened —

MAN: I'm not the kind of person who does things like that. Please. Don't go. Do what you need to do. I won't bother you. *(Beat.)* Maybe just . . . consider what I did a very warm Maine welcome?

WOMAN: *(Charmed.)* All right. All right. *(Beat.)* I'm — . My name's Glory.

MAN: I'm East.

GLORY: *(Confused.)*

EAST: For Easton. It's the name of the town — little ways that way — where I was born. Mess up on the birth certificate . . . "a son, *Easton*, born on this 6th day of January, 1969 in the town of Matthew, Maine" . . . instead of the other way around . . .

GLORY: *(Amused.)* Aw, I'm sorry . . . >

EAST: Naw . . .

GLORY: so, Easton, >

EAST: Yeah —

GLORY: yeah, I passed through there on my way here, and by the way, *(Scanning the horizon.)* where is "here," where am I? I couldn't find it on my map?

EAST: Um . . . Almost.

GLORY: What?

EAST: You're in unorganized territory. Township 13, Range 7. It's not gonna be on your map, 'cause it's not an actual town, technically. >

GLORY: What do you mean —

EAST: See, to be a town, you gotta get organized. And we never got around to getting' organized, so . . . we're just Almost.

GLORY: Oh . . .

(They enjoy this. Beat. Glory now deals with the fact that she is missing

her bag. She was clutching it to her chest, and now it's gone. This should upset her so much that it seems like it affects her breathing.)

GLORY: Oh! *(Like she can't breathe.)*

EAST: What?

GLORY: My heart!

EAST: What? Are you OK?

GLORY: My heart. *(Pointing to the bag.)*

EAST: What?

GLORY: You have my heart.

EAST: I —?

GLORY: In that bag, it's in that bag.

EAST: Oh.

GLORY: Please give it back, // please. It's my heart. I need it. Please.

EAST: OK. *(He gives her the bag.)*

GLORY: Thank you. *(Her breathing normalizes . . .)*

EAST: You're welcome.

    (A long beat while East considers what he has just heard.)

EAST: I'm sorry, did you just say that . . . your heart is in that bag?

GLORY: Yes.

EAST: *(Considers.)* It's heavy.

GLORY: Yes.

EAST: Why is it in that bag?

GLORY: It's how I carry it around.

EAST: Why?

GLORY: It's broken.

EAST: What happened?

GLORY: Wes broke it.

EAST: Your husband?

GLORY: Yeah. He went away. With someone else.

EAST: I'm sorry.

GLORY: Yeah. And when he did that, I felt like my heart would break. And that's exactly what happened. It broke: hardened up and cracked in two. Hurt so bad, I had to go to the hospital, and when I got there, they told me they were gonna have to take it out. And when they took it out, they dropped it on the floor and it broke into nineteen pieces. Slate. *(Shakes the bag, which should be filled with pieces of slate. Makes a great sound!)* It turned to slate.

EAST: *(Taking this in. His only response is:)* Great for roofing.

GLORY: *(Just looks at East.)*

EAST: *(Dawns on him.)* Wait a second, how do you breathe? If your heart is in that bag, how are you alive?

GLORY: *(Indicating the heart that's now in her chest.)* Artificial . . .

EAST: Really!?

GLORY: Yeah. 'Cause my real one's broken.

EAST: Then — why do you carry it *(the one in the bag)* around with you?

GLORY: It's my *heart.*

EAST: But it's broken.

GLORY: Yeah

EAST: 'Cause your husband left you.

GLORY: Yeah.

EAST: Well, why are you paying your respects to him if he left you?

GLORY: Because that's what you do when a person dies, you pay them respects —

EAST: But he left you.>

GLORY: Yeah, but —

EAST: and it seems to me that a man who leaves somebody doesn't deserve any respects . . . —

GLORY: Well, I just didn't leave things well with him, >

EAST: What do you mean?

GLORY: and I need to apologize to him.

EAST: But he left you!, >

GLORY: I know, but I —

EAST: why should you apologize?

GLORY: Because!

EAST: Because why?

GLORY: Because I killed him.

EAST: Oh.

GLORY: And I'd like to apologize. *(Beat. Then admission.)* See, he had come to visit me when I was in recovery from when they put my artificial heart in — I was almost better; I was just about to go home, too — and he said he wanted me back. And I said, "Wes, I have a new heart now. I'm sorry . . . It doesn't want you back . . ." And that just killed him.

EAST: Oh. *(Relief.)* But — you didn't *kill* him —

GLORY: Yes, I did! Because he got so sad that my new heart didn't want him back, he just tore outta the hospital, and . . . an ambulance that was comin' in from an emergency didn't see him and just . . . took him right out, and if I'd have been able to take him back, >

EAST: Glory —

GLORY: he wouldn't have torn outta there like that, >

EAST: Glory!

GLORY: and been just taken out like that, and so, I just feel that, for closure, the right thing to do is —

(East kisses Glory. When she pulls away, he has her heart again. She takes it back.)

GLORY: Please don't do that anymore.

EAST: I love you!

GLORY: Well, don't.

EAST: Why?

GLORY: Because I won't be able to love you back: I have a heart that can pump my blood and that's all. The one that does the other stuff is broken. It doesn't work anymore. *(Again, inexplicably drawn to her, he deliberately kisses her. He ends up with her heart again.)*

EAST: *(Re: her heart.)* Please let me have this.

GLORY: *(Trying to get her heart back.)* No! It's mine.

EAST: *(Keeping her heart.)* I can fix it!

GLORY: I don't know if I want you to!

EAST: Glory *(let me fix it.)* — !!!

GLORY: *(Going after her heart.)* East, please give that back to me.

EAST: *(Keeping her heart.)* But, it's broken. >

GLORY: Please — !

EAST: It's no good like this. >

GLORY: But, it's my heart, East!

EAST: *(Triumphantly.)* Yes, it is. And I believe I have it.

GLORY: *(This stops her.)*

EAST: . . . And I can fix it.

GLORY: *(No response — she's stuck.)*

EAST: I'm a repairman. I repair things. It's what I do.

(East starts to open the bag to examine its contents. As he opens the bag, music up, and the northern lights appear — in front of Glory, above Glory, on the field of stars behind Glory. Glory sees them . . . and they're a thing of wonder.)

GLORY: Oh! Oh, wow! Oh, wow! Oh, they're so beautiful . . . *(Remembering who they are.)* Oh! Oh! — Wes!! Wes!! Good-bye! I'm so sorry! . . . Good-bye, Wes!

(And the northern lights are gone. Glory looks at East, who has crouched down, taken a piece of her heart out of the bag, and is examining it. A beat. Then:)

GLORY: Hello, East.

(Music continues. East looks at Glory, and then he begins repairing her heart . . . as the lights fade to black.)

END OF SCENE

Almost, Maine
John Cariani

Seriocomic

Lendall and Gayle: twenties to thirties, but they could be almost any age

This play is about various denizens of a very small town somewhere in Maine, two of whom are Lendall and Gayle, a couple who may or may not be breaking up.

Note on symbols: The next character to speak should begin his or her line where the // appears in the speech of the character speaking. The symbol > appears at the end of a line that is not a complete thought. It means that the character speaking should drive through to the end of the thought, which will be continued in his or her next lines. Don't stop for the other character's line.

GETTING IT BACK

(Music fades. We hear someone pounding on a door.)

GAYLE: *(Pounding on the door.)* Lendall! *(More pounding.)* Lendall! *(More pounding.)* Lendall!

LENDALL: OK! Gayle! Shhh! I'm comin', I'm comin'.

GAYLE: Lendall!

LENDALL: Hey, hey, hey. Shh! *(Lendall exits stage left to answer the door.)*

GAYLE: *(Blowing by him.)* Lendall —

LENDALL: What's the matter?, what's goin' on?

GAYLE: *(Stewing.)*

LENDALL: What?

GAYLE: *(She's been in a bit of a state, but she collects herself.)* I want it back.

LENDALL: What?

GAYLE: I want it back.

LENDALL: What?

GAYLE: All the love I gave to you?, I want it back.

LENDALL: What?

GAYLE: *Now.*

LENDALL: Why?

GAYLE: I've got yours in the car.

LENDALL: What?

GAYLE: All the love you gave to me?, I've got it in the car.

LENDALL: Well, why do you —

GAYLE: I don't want it anymore.

LENDALL: Why?

GAYLE: I've made a decision: We're done.

LENDALL: What? —

GAYLE: We're done. I've decided. And, so, I've brought all the love you gave to me back to you. It's the right thing to do.

LENDALL: *(Bewildered.)* Um, I —

GAYLE: It's in the car.

LENDALL: You said. *(He's kind of paralyzed trying to figure this out.)*

GAYLE: *(Waiting for him to take some action, and go get the love.)* I can get it *for* you, or . . . *you* can get it.

LENDALL: Well, I don't want it back. I don't need it —

GAYLE: Well, *I* don't want it. What am I supposed to do with all of it, now that I don't want it?

LENDALL: Well, I don't know . . .

GAYLE: Well, under the circumstances //, it doesn't seem right for me to keep it, so I'm gonna give it back. *(She leaves.)*

LENDALL: Under what circumstances? *(Calling to her.)* Gayle — what are — I don't understand what — . . . What are you doing?

GAYLE: *(Offstage.)* I told you. I'm getting all the love you gave to me and I'm giving it back to you.

LENDALL: *(Calling to her.)* Well, I'm not sure I want it — Whoah! Need help?

GAYLE: Nope. I got it. It's not heavy.
(Gayle returns with a huge, red bag full of love. The bag should be filled with balloons or foam or pillow stuffing or something. She places it on the floor. Beat.)

GAYLE: Here you go.

LENDALL: *(Truly puzzled, referring to the bag of love.)* And this is . . . ?

GAYLE: All the love you gave me.

LENDALL: Wow. *(Beat.)* That's a *lot. (Gayle exits and returns with some more bags of love.)*

GAYLE: Yeah.

LENDALL: Whole lot.

GAYLE: Yeah. *(Gayle exits and returns with an even larger number of bags of love. There is now a huge pile of love on the floor.)*

LENDALL: Wow. What the heck am I gonna do with all that? I mean . . . I don't know if I have room.

GAYLE: *(Upset.)* I'm sure you'll find a place for it *(i.e., another woman.)* . . . And now, I think it's only fair for you to give me mine back because . . . I want it back. *(Beat.)* All the love I gave to you?

LENDALL: Yeah?

GAYLE: I want it back. *(Beat.)* So go get it.

LENDALL: *(He doesn't go get it. He's probably trying to figure out why all this is happening.)*

GAYLE: Lendall, go get it. Please. *Now!!!*

(Beat.)

LENDALL: OK.

(Lendall exits. Gayle sits in the chair and waits. Lendall returns with a teeny-tiny little bag — a little pouch — and places it on a little table next to the chair. They look at the little bag. The bag should be between Lendall and Gayle. And Gayle should be between the many bags of love and the little bag of love.)

GAYLE: What is that?

LENDALL: *(It's obvious — it's exactly what she asked for.)* It's all the love you gave me.

GAYLE: That's *(all the love I gave to you)?* — . . . That is *not* — . . . there is no way . . . that is *not* — *(Realizing how little of it there is.)* Is that all I gave you?

LENDALL: It's all I could find . . .

GAYLE: Oh. OK. OK.

(They look at the little bag, and then at all the big bags; Gayle is upset.)

LENDALL: Gayle . . . What's goin' on, here?

GAYLE: I told you: We're done.

LENDALL: Why do you keep saying that? —

GAYLE: Because — *(Very hard to say, but it has to be said.)* Because when

I asked you if you ever thought we were gonna get married —
remember when I asked you that?, in December? . . . It was
snowing? . . .

LENDALL: Yeah.

GAYLE: Yeah, well, when I asked you . . . *that,* you got so . . . *quiet.* And
everybody said that that right there // shoulda told me everything —

LENDALL: Everybody *who?*

GAYLE: Everybody!

LENDALL: Who?

GAYLE: . . . Marvalyn >

LENDALL: *Marvalyn?*!? Marvalyn said that — like she's an expert? — . . .

GAYLE: said — yes, Marvalyn, yes, said that how quiet you got was all I
needed to know, and she's right: You don't love me.

LENDALL: What — ? Gayle, no!

GAYLE: Shh! And I've been trying to fix that, I've tried to *make* you love
me by giving you every bit of love I had, and now . . . I don't have
any love for *me* left, and that's . . . that's not good for a person . . .
and . . . that's why I want all the love I gave you back, because I wanna
bring it with me.

LENDALL: Where are you going?

GAYLE: I need to get away from things.

LENDALL: What — ? What things?! There aren't any things in this town
to get away from . . .

GAYLE: Yes there are: you.

LENDALL: Me?

GAYLE: Yes. *You* are the things in this town I need to get away from because I have to think and start over, and so: All the love I gave to you?
I want it back, in case I need it. Because I can't very well go around
giving *your love* — 'cause that's all I have right now, is the love *you*
gave *me* — I can't very well go around giving *your* love to other guys,
'cause —

LENDALL: Other *guys?* There are other guys?!?

GAYLE: No, not yet, but I'm assuming there *will* be.

LENDALL: Gayle —

GAYLE: Shh! — So I think — . I think that, since I know now that you're not ready to do what comes next for people who have been together for quite a long time *(i.e., get married.)*, I think we're gonna be done, >

LENDALL: Why, Gayle? We're a team!

GAYLE: and so, I think the best thing we can do now, is just return the love we gave to each other and call it . . . *(Taking in the bags — the pathetic one that contains the love she gave him, and the awesome several that contain the love he gave her.)* . . . even *(it's not "even" at all)* . . . Oh, Jeezum Crow, is that really all the love I gave you, Lendall? I mean, I thought — . I mean what kind of person am I if this is all the love I gave y — . . . No . . . no-no-no . . . *(Fiercely.)* I *know* I gave you more than that, Lendall, I *know* it! *(She thinks. Collects herself. New attack.)* Did you lose it?

LENDALL: No, Gayle —

GAYLE: Did you lose it, Lendall? 'Cause I know I gave you more than that and I think you're pulling something on me, and this is not a good time to be pulling something on me —

LENDALL: I'm not. Pulling something on you. I wouldn't do that to you . . . Just — I think — . . . Gosh — . . . I think you should just take what you came for and I guess I'll see you later. *(This is pretty final. He exits into the rest of the house.)*

GAYLE: *(Realization of the finality. Calls him, weakly.)* Lendall . . . Lendall . . . *(She is at a loss. But this is what she wants. She looks at the little bag, takes it, and is about to leave. But she stops, sits in the chair, opens it . . . and examines what's inside.)* Lendall? What is this? What the heck is this, Lendall? This is *not* the love I gave you, Lendall, at least have the decency to give me back what *(I gave you)* — . Lendall, what is this?

LENDALL: *(Returning.)* It's a ring, Gayle.

GAYLE: What?

LENDALL: It's a ring.

GAYLE: Well — this isn't — *(the love I gave you).* This is *not (the love I gave you —* . . . *(She gets it.)* Oh, Lendall, this is a ring! Is this a . . . ring? A ring that you give to someone you've been with for quite a long time if you want to let them know that you're ready to do what comes next for people who have been together for quite a long time . . . ?

LENDALL: Mmhmm.

GAYLE: Oh . . . Oh . . . *(Beat.)* But . . . all the love I gave to you? Where is it?

LENDALL: It's right there, Gayle. *(Referring to the ring.)*

GAYLE: But —

LENDALL: It's right there.

GAYLE: But —

LENDALL: It *is.* That's it. Right there. There was so much of it — you gave me so much, over the years —

GAYLE: *Eleven.*

LENDALL: — over the eleven years —

GAYLE: *Eleven,* yeah.

LENDALL: — yeah, you gave me so much that I didn't know what to do with it all. I had to put some in the garage, some in the shed. I asked my dad if he had any suggestions what to do with it all, and he said, "You got a ring yet?" I said, "No." And he said, "Get her one. When there's that much of that stuff comin' in, that's about the only place you can put it." *(Beat.)* He said it'd all fit. *(i.e., in the ring.) (Beat.)* And he was right. *(Beat. They look at the ring.)* That thing is a lot bigger than it looks . . .

(Beat.)

LENDALL: So, there it is. All the love you gave to me. Just not in the same . . . form as when you gave it . . .

GAYLE: Yeah.

(Beat.)

LENDALL: You still want it back?

GAYLE: Yes. I do.

LENDALL: Well, then . . . take it.

GAYLE: *(She takes the ring out of the box. Then:)* Can I keep all that? *(Referring to the laundry bags full of love he gave to her.)*

LENDALL: It's yours.

GAYLE: Thank you.

(Lendall puts the ring on Gayle's finger. Music.)

GAYLE: Lendall — You didn't have to get me a ring. That's not what I was asking —

LENDALL: Yes I did. It was time. And it's honorable.

GAYLE: Well . . . it's very beautiful. *(Beat.)* Lendall — . . . I'm sorry! It's just — it's a Friday night and I was sittin' home all by myself and I started thinkin' and —

LENDALL: *(Kissing her.)* Shh . . .

(Lendall takes Gayle's hand. They dance. Gayle stops, suddenly — upon seeing the bags of love.)

GAYLE: Lendall . . . what the heck are we gonna do with all that? *(Referring to the bags of love.)*

LENDALL: I don't know. 'Cause there's a whole lot more where that came from . . .

GAYLE: *(A suggestion of sex, babies, and her own expanding happiness.)* Well . . . we're gonna need a lot more room, mister.

(Music. Lendall takes Gayle's hand. They dance. Lights fade to black.)

END OF SCENE

Bulrusher
Eisa Davis

Dramatic
Bulrusher and Boy, teens

> *Bulrusher is a mixed-race girl who is something of a clairvoyant. The boy (White) is sweet on her.*
>
> *Note: Much use is made in the play of a dialect called "Boontling." A glossary of terms is contained in the complete text of the play (see Rights and Permissions page in the rear of this volume for details).*

BOY: Where'd you get that moshe?

BULRUSHER: I ain't talkin' to you.

BOY: Your truck. Where'd you get it. Where'd you get it?

BULRUSHER: While back I got it.

BOY: Where from? Truck like that just don't fall on you. You musta finagled it some kinda way. I want me a truck. Always hitchin' a ride to see my ma in Mendocino — I want me a truck a my own.

BULRUSHER: Yeah, well.

BOY: You got one. I can do as good as you, or better. Get me a new one. Goddamn I need a cigarette. You got a cigarette?

BULRUSHER: You want a cigarette?

BOY: Yeah.

BULRUSHER: They're inside the house.

BOY: Wait. I forgot. You my new girlfriend. I gotta be nice. I pretty please pretty face need a pretty cigarette. Please.

BULRUSHER: I'm getting 'em anyway. I'm headed into Cloverdale, pick up my oranges.

(She goes in, but peeks out at him through the window.)

BOY: *(Sings.)* Thorn, spine and thistle
Bramble, pennywhistle
Poisoned flowers on a vine

Sticky cockleburrs and pine
Sap that's sweet but never kind
Stuck like so much gristle
(Calls to her.)
I made that one up. What kinda perfume you use?

BULRUSHER: *(Offstage.)* I don't.

BOY: There's a smell I smell when I come near ya.
(She comes back onto porch. She has no cigarettes.)

BULRUSHER: Orange rind.

BOY: No, sweeter.

BULRUSHER: Algae.

BOY: Come on now, say something pretty.

BULRUSHER: Fresh out.

BOY: No pretty words and no cigs? Well. Just looking at you smokes me.

BULRUSHER: Be seein' ya.

BOY: *(New tack.)* Every Monday you head into Cloverdale. Pick up your oranges, sell 'em to the town. You must make you a lot of money. What you do with it?

BULRUSHER: Well I ain't givin' none to you. I'll be gettin' on the road.

BOY: The pike!

BULRUSHER: *Road.*

BOY: *Pike.* You harp the ling, maybe people would like you.

BULRUSHER: They buy my oranges. That's enough.

BOY: Schoolch won't let you talk the way we all talk, huh.

BULRUSHER: Don't need to.

BOY: You can't find out anything 'bout anyone in this town if you don't harp the ling. Like last night. I found out why that McGimsey girl went mossy on me — she's been bilchin' Tom Soo, and his ma is Chinese! that ain't so bad, but Tom Soo? Tom Soo from Philo? She ain't had a taste for any tarp but boarch, so I'm glad she got ink-standy with me. Can't have no applehead ruinin' my track record, sunderin' my reputation. I'm a standin' man.

BULRUSHER: I reckon.

BOY: I ain't afraid a talkin' to you. Hey, I just splashed in this bowl a water.

BULRUSHER: Yeah.

BOY: Means my fortune's in it. You could stick your fingers in there and tell what's gon' happen to me. What's my life gonna feel like? What's it gonna feel like when I touch you?

(He reaches for her arm. She lets him touch her, then pulls away.)

BULRUSHER: I only tell the weather now. Ain't read nobody's bathwater in years. After the May Bloyd incident.

BOY: It was you brought that on May Bloyd?

BULRUSHER: I just told her it was coming.

BOY: And you never read nobody since.

BULRUSHER: Sometimes I get a little taste by accident. Like in the general store and one of the twins hand me a coke got beads of water on the bottle.

BOY: Con-den-sa-tion is the proper name.

BULRUSHER: Con-des-cen-sion, I'll try to remember that.

BOY: So you're smart too.

BULRUSHER: Don't try to school the schoolteacher's girl.

BOY: You're so smart, you oughta tell fortunes again. Get you a booth at the Apple Show.

BULRUSHER: I said I ain't done it in years.

BOY: So you can't do it anymore.

BULRUSHER: I'm at the peak of my perception! I can call rain a whole week off from it coming down. I'm the best I've ever been.

BOY: And keepin' it all to yourself. People come from all over the country for the Apple Show. You could make a name with folks you never even met. You need you a manager, to publicize all your ventures. You could really make a killing.

BULRUSHER: For what?

BOY: I don't know. Why you think you got that power in the first place?

(Bulrusher starts to go.)

BOY: Look, you could just tell my fortune then.

BULRUSHER: I ain't putting my fingers in there. Or your bathwater.

BOY: What about spit? That's water, right? If you just kiss me you'll know everything there is to know.

BULRUSHER: One of your friends put you up to this? You messin' with me just 'cause everyone thinks you're cute? Just 'cause you can?

BOY: Tiger lily, manzanita, you're my girlfriend. *(Sings.)* Oh my girl —

BULRUSHER: If I'm your girlfriend, prove it. Give me something.

BOY: I ain't got much to offer a girl except my sensuality. We could take a walk through Fern Canyon, watch the salmon run —

BULRUSHER: It's summertime, ain't no salmon running the river.

BOY: There's always trout. Steelhead trout.

BULRUSHER: Take me somewhere where there's people and put your arm around me. Take me to the Anyhow.

BOY: The Anyhow Saloon? I just came from there.

BULRUSHER: And I'm leavin' here.

(Bulrusher opens the door to her truck.)

BOY: Come on, tiger lily, you never told me where you got your truck.

BULRUSHER: You don't want to know.

BOY: You steal it?

BULRUSHER: No.

BOY: Then where'd you get it?

BULRUSHER: *(Suddenly flaring.)* Where'd I get my truck? Where'd I get my truck? From a Pomo Indian, that's where.

BOY: A Indian?

BULRUSHER: Come up to the gas station in this red truck, said he left the reservation near Clear Lake and is gonna walk all the way down the coast to Mexico.

BOY: Come on now —

BULRUSHER: *(Interrupting.)* I said that's nice, what you gon' do with your truck. He said "It's yours. My wife is dead and I don't need it."

BOY: Wait, how's that follow?

BULRUSHER: Listen steada talking and you might find out. I asked him what his wife die of. Me, he said. She couldn't stand me. And he said it to me just like this: "Used to leave me every weekend. Just get in the truck and drive off. I'd have to call Earl for a ride and we'd find her on the cliffs. She said it was sacred ground and the grey whales knew it. They'd stop in that tiny bay there and blow all night long. Sprayin' air over the grounds where our people used to live in the old days. She'd cry, just touch a tree and cry. Cry and say that we had nothing left, not even spirit, that we were all just junkyards of tin cans and rubber tires. Say that she'd jump in the ocean if Earl and me got any closer. So we'd sit and let her cry to the whales and smear sand in her hair and dance on the heather there on the bluffs.

Took her back home after a while, but she just kept sayin' she was tired of the new ways and couldn't we just live somewhere sacred again and if we didn't I was a coward afraid ta leave my mom on the Rez and I said we are already sacred. We are walking spirit. Don't discount your own body as land that is what it is and it is a desecration to say it is anything less but she snuck my gun into that truck, drove off one night to the bluffs and I don't know if she shot herself or if she got hit with the killer waves but she was gone when Earl and I came to find her and the shotgun was on the heather. So I'm going to Mexico. I'm gonna walk, pay for her life with my blisters. She knows I mean to have her and her anger with me every inch of the way down to Mexico. I don't think love can shoot time, I don't think love can murder all the hours we spend alone, and I wish it would, that love I had, love that blows like a grey whale on a dark summer night headin' back up to Arctic cold — yes. I stopped here to fill up my truck, but I don't need it. You take it." And he started to walk.

That what you wanted to know?

BOY: I guess. Free truck. Whoo, you got good luck. Can you give me some?

(Bulrusher gets into her truck and slams the door.)

BOY: Bulrusher, be my fortune.

(Boy dumps the bowl of water on his head.)

(Sings:) Oh my girl, with the cattail curls, be mine, be mine, all mine.

(Bulrusher drives along the river and talks to it.)

BULRUSHER: Where'd I get my truck? That's his pickup line? Where'd I get my truck. I'm a bulrusher. So no one but me could have taken that truck. Heartbreak is where I live, my misery a prescription for everyone else's comfort. People who are hurt, or want to be, come to me because they see I hold more hurt than they can and still got room for theirs. I never read that Indian man's water, but he probably walked all the way down to Mexico. I suppose it's in my best interest to think so, 'cause I like my pickup. It's a flatbed. Red.

END OF SCENE

Cowboy Versus Samurai
Michael Golamco

Comic
Travis and Veronica, twenties to thirties

> *Travis and Veronica are two of the only three Asian Americans living in a small town in Wyoming. Veronica only dates Caucasians, much to the dismay of Travis, who is sweet on her.*

TRAVIS: *(Recalls)* Donald Dabbraccio, Ryan Perkins, Todd O'Reilly. I see a pattern here.

VERONICA: Yes. You only go out with Asian women.

TRAVIS: I was going to say that you only go out with D —

VERONICA: Don't start.

TRAVIS: Don't start what?

VERONICA: The lecture you're about to give me.

TRAVIS: I was just going to point out a particular taste in men that you have.

VERONICA: And what is that?

TRAVIS: Oh, I don't know —

VERONICA: I just get along better with, and I've always only been attracted to —

TRAVIS AND VERONICA TOGETHER: White guys —

VERONICA: Yes, and that's my business.

TRAVIS: Yeah, but why is that?

VERONICA: I don't know.

TRAVIS: You've never dated an Asian guy?

VERONICA: I have. Once.

TRAVIS: Well I tried broccoli once, and I was sorta disappointed but I gave it a second chance.

VERONICA: Travis, does this bother you? You're acting as if this bothers you.

TRAVIS: Of course it bothers me. It's like when four out of five dentists recommend a brand of toothpaste. I'm like the crappy brand that the fifth guy recommends.

VERONICA: Look — it's what I'm used to and what I'm attracted to. And it's nobody's business —

TRAVIS: Fine.

VERONICA: So is that all right with you?

TRAVIS: Yeah.

VERONICA: Travis —

TRAVIS: No, it's fine with me.

VERONICA: Good. Because I don't want to find out that you're going to judge me just because of my likes and dislikes.

TRAVIS: All right. But for your information, I want you to know that I don't just date Asian women. I'm all over the color spectrum.

VERONICA: Oh yeah?

TRAVIS: Yeah. I once had this long, amazing relationship with this incredible Puerto Rican girl. A gymnast. Though I had to break it off with her when I found out that she had a fetish for Asian men.

VERONICA: Really?

TRAVIS: Yeah. She used to clip pictures out of *Martial Artist Magazine.*

VERONICA: Come on — we'd better get started on dinner. Let's see you work your magic.

TRAVIS: All right.

(As she exits —)

VERONICA: You make me feel good, Travis. I move out here to the middle of nowhere, and I still find someone to eat tofu with.

END OF SCENE

Cul-De-Sac
John Cariani

Seriocomic

Jill and Roger Johnson, probably thirties, but they could be any age

The Johnsons' marriage is in a rut, and they are finding themselves increasingly envious of their neighbors, the Joneses.

(Jill and Roger Johnson's kitchen. Jill enters her home, via the side door — which leads into the kitchen. She backs in. We hear a car drive up. This is Jill's husband, Roger, coming home from work. Roger is sad — absorbed by his sadness. Jill continues looking out the window.)
   Note on symbols: The next character to speak should begin his or her line where the // appears in the speech of the character speaking. The symbol > appears at the end of a line that is not a complete thought. It means that the character speaking should drive through to the end of the thought, which will be continued in his or her next lines. Don't stop for the other character's line.

ROGER: Hey.

JILL: Hey. *(Looking out the window.)*
   (Beat.)

ROGER: So . . . honey — . . . I didn't call. I'm sorry I didn't call, but I didn't call because . . . I *couldn't*, because . . . I didn't get it. *(He looks at her — but she's looking out the window.)* Honey.

JILL: *(Finally turning to him.)* Hmm?

ROGER: I said I'd call you either way and I didn't and I'm sorry I didn't — but I didn't because I didn't get it. I was . . . passed over, they said.

JILL: I thought maybe.

ROGER: How'd // you — ?

JILL: You didn't call.

ROGER: I couldn't. I'm sorry.

(Beat. Jill turns back to the window.)

ROGER: They gave me a title change.

JILL: Hm.

ROGER: A promotion in name only, they call it. But it's not, really. A promotion. Just a renaming of what I already do.

JILL: Uh-huh. I'm sorry.

(Beat.)

ROGER: You should hug me. Instead of staring out the window, what are you doing, anyway, staring out the window like that? You should . . . give me a — . . .

(Jill hugs Roger.)

ROGER: . . . hug. *(He relaxes.)* Thanks. *(He is very happy to receive the hug.)* *(Jill goes back to the window — doesn't listen to the following.)*

ROGER: It's weird. I was so shocked and then just . . . sad. And then angry. *(Beat.)* I left early. Went for a drive. Thought things I've never thought before, you know? When something like this happens — when you just don't get what you always thought you'd get — you start to understand why people, you know, do some of the crazy things they do in this world — . . . *(Notices his wife is just staring out the window — not listening to him.)* Hey.

JILL: *(No answer.)*

ROGER: Honey.

JILL: *(Still fixated on something outside.)* Hmm?

ROGER: I'm talking.

JILL: *(No answer.)*

ROGER: What're you doing?

JILL: Huh?

ROGER: What? What's goin' — . . . Somethin' goin' on next door?

JILL: No.

ROGER: You're lookin' awfully absorbed for there to be nothin' // goin' on . . .

JILL: I'm sorry, no, no, I'm just thinkin'.

ROGER: About what?

JILL: Just . . . the Joneses.

ROGER: Oh. Well, what about 'em?

JILL: Do you think we're keeping up with them?

ROGER: What?

JILL: Do you think we're keeping up with them?

ROGER: Wha — ? Well — honey, I don't know. Why?

JILL: 'Cause they're just doing so . . . *well.* Did you see their new cars? His and hers.

ROGER: *(This stops him. He goes to the window to look.)* Yeah. I did. *(They covet the cars.)* You know how fast those things can go?

JILL: No.

ROGER: Fast.

JILL: Oh. *(Beat.)* Irene said that Joe bought 'em to help them feel like they used to feel.

ROGER: Oh. Well, how did they used to feel?

JILL: Like dreamers.

ROGER: Oh.

JILL: Like they could go anywhere and do anything.

ROGER: Oh.

> *(Beat. They ponder this.)*

JILL: Irene said that hers is the color Joe had in his head when he first saw her. And Joe's is the color Irene had in her head when she first saw him.

ROGER: Oh.

JILL: Custom.

ROGER: Hmm?

JILL: Paint jobs. // Paint jobs are custom.

ROGER: Oh, yeah, I was wondering about those . . . *colors.*

JILL: Yeah.

> *(Beat.)*

JILL: Honey . . .

ROGER: What?

JILL: Just — did you have a color in your head when you first saw me?

ROGER: Um . . . I don't know. I don't remember. >

JILL: Me neither.

ROGER: Did you have one in your head for me?

JILL: No, I don't remember, either.

> *(Beat.)*

JILL: Anyway, they're really happy about 'em, Irene said.

ROGER: Hmm?

JILL: The cars. Irene just told me that they're really happy about 'em.

ROGER: Oh, well . . they should be. They're nice cars. I'd be pretty happy, too, if I had a car like that.

JILL: Happier than you are now?

ROGER: Well, yeah, probably, seeing how today wasn't exactly the best day of my life. I mean — a car like that? Be better than driving a *sedan* . . .

JILL: I bet they're probably even happier now than they were before they got the cars.

ROGER: Yeah. Probably.

JILL: You think?

ROGER: Yeah. I mean, I think Joe and Irene are pretty happy people in general, with or without the cars, but >

JILL: Happier than us?

ROGER: the cars help, I'm sure, with // their general happiness —

JILL: Happier than us?

ROGER: What?

JILL: Do you think the Joneses are happier than us? // Now that they have those cars?

ROGER: Well, what kind of — . I don't know, 'cause I don't know how happy they are, >

JILL: Oh — they're very happy.

ROGER: only *they* know how happy they are, // if they're even happy at all.

JILL: They're very happy, very happy.

ROGER: Well, yeah, maybe, but we don't know that, // we can't know that for sure —

JILL: Oh, no: we know! Everyone knows. The whole neighborhood knows. >

ROGER: Well —

JILL: They're happy.

ROGER: I'm not saying they're *not* happy, honey! I'm just saying that that we'll never really know if they're happy or if they're not, so, why worry about it? Let's just worry about us being happy. I mean, that's all that matters to me, is that we're happy. *(Kiss.)* And I think we are.

JILL: Yeah?

ROGER: Yeah.

JILL: How can you tell?

ROGER: Well, you smile. A lot.

JILL: Mm. Yeah, I do.

ROGER: And people generally smile when they're happy.

JILL: I guess.

ROGER: So . . . that leads me to believe that you're happy. And I'm —
today being an exception — I'm a pretty happy guy, so I would say
we're happy. *(Beat.)* And if we're not, we should be, because it's encouraged. >

JILL: Encouraged?

ROGER: In fact, that's what I kept telling myself on my way home from
work, that I gotta find a way to be happy — even though I'm
not — because I live in a place where it's encouraged.

JILL: What's encouraged?

ROGER: Happiness. Being happy. We're encouraged to be happy.

JILL: Who is?

ROGER: All of us.

JILL: By who?

ROGER: Huh?

JILL: Who encourages us to be happy?

ROGER: Well, the guy who wrote a long time ago that that's what we would
get to do with our lives: have the right to live, and be free, and be
happy, // and —

JILL: Pursue.

ROGER: What?

JILL: It's *pursue* happy.

ROGER: What?

JILL: We don't have the right to *be* happy. We have the right to *pursue*
happy. You said *be* happy.

ROGER: Well —

JILL: It's "life, liberty, and the *pursuit* of happiness." We only get to
chase it.

ROGER: Well —

JILL: And they seem to have caught it, they've captured it.

ROGER: What?, Who?

JILL: The Joneses. They seem to have successfully pursued it and captured it. *(Off his confusion.)* Happiness. They're just happy people. They're well-suited to it.

ROGER: Well, who's not well-suited to // being happy?

JILL: No — I just mean — they're very good at it, at being happy in the world we've made. They are so good at happily going about doing what people usually do. They've figured out how to live the life we've all chosen to lead with such grace. >

ROGER: Yeah, I guess they have —

JILL: And they do it so happily.

ROGER: Well —

JILL: They are happy people, honey. >

ROGER: Well, yeah,

JILL: I know. I watch. I see.

ROGER: and that's good, isn't it? I mean, that's all you can hope for for people is that they're happy. Right?

END OF SCENE

Cul-De-Sac
John Cariani

Seriocomic

Christy and James Smith, probably thirties, but they could be any age

> *Christy, a housewife, suffers from depression, and she spends most of her days in bed. Today, though, she's had a good day. She got up! And went out! James, her husband, is thrilled.*
>
> *Note on symbols: The next character to speak should begin his or her line where the // appears in the speech of the character speaking. The symbol > appears at the end of a line that is not a complete thought. It means that the character speaking should drive through to the end of the thought, which will be continued in his or her next lines. Don't stop for the other character's line.*

> *(Christy and James Smith's bedroom. Christy is lying on her bed, maybe asleep, maybe staring out the window — which faces the Jones' house. I think she stirs or starts to get up — like she doesn't want to be caught in bed — during the previous scene between James and Joe. Maybe she tries to get up. We hear James enter. She tries — not very successfully — to pull herself together, make the bed, maybe.)*
> *(James enters and goes to window, and looks out at the Jones'.)*

[JOE: Honey, I'm home.]

> *(James sees Irene greet Joe — Joe and Irene hug and kiss, probably pretty passionately. Maybe they feel they're being watched and they pull the curtains shut? Beat.)*

JAMES: *(He tries what Joe did, to see if he gets the same response from his wife.)* Honey, I'm home. *(No dice.)*

CHRISTY: *(No answer — is she sleeping?)*

JAMES: *(Going into the bedroom.)* Honey, I'm home.

CHRISTY: *(Getting up, covering.)* Hey, how was your day? >

JAMES: Good —

CHRISTY: How was your meeting, >

JAMES: Good, honey —

CHRISTY: you had that meeting, right?

JAMES: Yeah —

CHRISTY: And the luncheon, how was your luncheon? >

JAMES: Fine, honey —

CHRISTY: Was it a late luncheon, 'cause, >

JAMES: What were you doing? >

CHRISTY: well, I hope you're hungry, >

JAMES: were you in bed?

CHRISTY: are you hungry, 'cause I am starving!

JAMES: I'm starving, actually, too, but —

CHRISTY: Well, then, I'm gonna make us a nice dinner —

JAMES: but, were you in bed? >

CHRISTY: What? No! No!

JAMES: You look like you were in bed, >

CHRISTY: No! No!

JAMES: were you?

CHRISTY: No! I was up! // And dressed!

JAMES: Are you sure?

CHRISTY: Yeah!

JAMES: 'Cause you look like you were in bed —

CHRISTY: I was up!

JAMES: Well, you better have been, 'cause —

CHRISTY: Honey! I'm up, I was up!

JAMES: OK — you just don't look like it.

CHRISTY: Well, I'm up! I was up! *(Conceding.)* I was just tired, I wanted to lie down.

JAMES: *(Taking this in, accusing.)* So you *weren't* up!

CHRISTY: Well . . . it was just a nap.

JAMES: Well, you gotta start gettin' up and stayin' up. 'Cause I get home and I'm starving . . .

CHRISTY: I know, I know, honey. //I know you're starving, I am too!

JAMES: And you gotta at least have dinner ready for me —

CHRISTY: I'm gonna! *Have* dinner ready for you!

JAMES: When I get home, though, when I get home, that's the least you can do: I go out there and get us the stuff and the things we need to survive and you can stay inside as long as you need to, but only if you start takin' the steps you need to take to help us get back to being what we used to be, >

CHRISTY: I know —

JAMES: and feeling like we used to feel, >

CHRISTY: I know —

JAMES: and one of those steps is . . . makin' us dinner, us havin' dinner together . . . >

CHRISTY: What?

JAMES: You gotta start kissin' me.

CHRISTY: Hon —

JAMES: I'm just home from work. You should kiss me. Like Irene just did.

CHRISTY: Like Irene just did?

JAMES: Yeah. She just kissed Joe when he came home from work the way a man would want his wife to kiss him at the end of a long hard day at work.

CHRISTY: Oh.

JAMES: Like — a big wet one, like they haven't seen each other in forever or something.

CHRISTY: Oh.

JAMES: And it hasn't been forever. It's been a few hours. A workday.

CHRISTY: Yeah.

JAMES: They did the same thing this morning on their way to work.

CHRISTY: Oh?

JAMES: Yeah.

(Beat.)

JAMES: Lotta love in that house. *(And not a lot of love in this one.)*

CHRISTY: Yeah.

(Beat. They stare at the Jones' house.)

JAMES: You gotta start doin' that again.

CHRISTY: What?

JAMES: Kissin' me.

CHRISTY: Yeah.

JAMES: When I come home from work.

CHRISTY: Yeah.

JAMES: Like you used to.

CHRISTY: Yeah.

JAMES: It's what people do.

CHRISTY: You're right.

> *(I think there is a kiss here — just on the cheek. James goes for more — but Christy shrinks away.)*

JAMES: Thanks. So . . . wanna just get a pizza?, >

CHRISTY: What? No —

JAMES: since you didn't have dinner ready — I mean, it's OK — we could just get a pizza.

CHRISTY: Oh, honey, no! I've taken care of — I've got a nice dinner planned, I really do —

JAMES: I mean, if you could just do that — kiss me and have dinner ready for me every day when I come from work from now on — even if it's just a pizza, like Irene does for Joe — I'll do something about the lawn!

CHRISTY: What?

JAMES: The lawn. I've really let it go.

CHRISTY: Oh.

JAMES: It's so brown and patchy.

CHRISTY: Oh.

JAMES: We've never let it go so bad. I mean, the Jones' is so green. So lush.

CHRISTY: Lush?

JAMES: And green, right?

CHRISTY: Yeah, I guess.

JAMES: I mean, look at *it* >

CHRISTY: I'm lookin', I'm lookin' —

JAMES: and look at ours. I mean, it's just the other side of the fence, but it's so *green. (Beat.)* Always has been. *(Beat.)* I keep noticing that lately. And it's buggin' me.

CHRISTY: Well, honey, we don't put that much effort into lawn care, so . . . >

JAMES: True.

CHRISTY: it shouldn't *bug* you.

JAMES: It does though.

CHRISTY: Well, if it bugs you, you should do something about it.

JAMES: Like what?

CHRISTY: Well, like lime.

JAMES: What?

CHRISTY: Lime. You gotta lime it.

JAMES: That's what Joe just said.

CHRISTY: Yeah, somethin' about the soil here. Changes the pH.

JAMES: The what?

CHRISTY: How acidic it is. You gotta lime it. Takes more than just an occasional mow.

JAMES: How'd you know that?

CHRISTY: Saw it on one of the shows on one of the channels.

JAMES: Oh.

(Beat.)

JAMES: I'd love a lawn like that. Like the Jones'.

CHRISTY: Well, then you should get some lime, // honey, I — .

JAMES: Yeah. I guess I oughta. *(He goes.)*

CHRISTY: Where you goin'?

JAMES: Get some lime. You did your part. You kissed me. Now I'll do mine. We can't have our lawn lookin' like this. Not when the Jones' is like that.

CHRISTY: Well, I didn't mean you oughta do it now. Why don't you wait till after dinner, I was gonna make us a nice dinner, 'cause —

JAMES: Oh — you know what — don't worry about it. It'll take too long to make. Let's just order a pizza. It's Friday. We usually order in on Fridays, pizza, usually, right?

CHRISTY: Well, yeah, but — I thought we might want to do something a little different tonight — // I thought I'd . . .

JAMES: *(Big new idea!)* Do you wanna go out?

(Little beat.)

CHRISTY: What?

JAMES: Do you wanna go out?

CHRISTY: Well —

JAMES: For dinner?

CHRISTY: Hon —

JAMES: Do you think you'd be up for that?

CHRISTY: No, no, I don't know — I mean —

JAMES: 'Cause I'm starving. Let's go out!

CHRISTY: But I went to some trouble, honey, I went to the trouble of putting together a nice dinner for us —

JAMES: *(Turning to window.)* I think we should. I really think we should. Go out. Together. Somewhere.

CHRISTY: Honey —

JAMES: 'Cause we don't go anywhere or do anything anymore.

CHRISTY: I know —

JAMES: And the Joneses do. They go places and do things. That's why they got those cars — did you see their new cars?

CHRISTY: Yeah —

JAMES: Yeah, they got 'em so they could do anything and go anywhere. Fast.

CHRISTY: Oh.

(Little beat.)

JAMES: *(Turning to window.)* Let's go out to dinner! We used to be so hungry on Friday nights, remember? Let's go to Sal's! >

CHRISTY: Honey —

JAMES: Quick! Before you can even think about why it is you hate it out there so much!

CHRISTY: Honey, I don't want to go to Sal's // I got us salmon!

JAMES: But I think we've gotta get you goin' out there again. We gotta go out. Somewhere. Together. Or at least *do* something. Together. We don't do anything. *(To window.)* The Joneses dance on Friday nights.

CHRISTY: How do you know?

JAMES: I've been watching.

CHRISTY: You shouldn't do that, it's creepy.

JAMES: But we don't do anything. I just sit here. And you just lie there . . . It's time to stop.

CHRISTY: I know. I know. And I *did!* I stopped // today.

JAMES: I mean, do you remember what we used to be?

CHRISTY: Barely.

JAMES: It wasn't this.

CHRISTY: I know.

(Beat.)

JAMES: I mean, everybody needs help once in a while, remembering what they *were,* how they used to feel together, finding what they've . . .

lost. Even the Joneses — as great as they are — even they need to try to remember what they were. That's why Joe said he got those cars, he said. To help them feel like they used to feel.

CHRISTY: Really?

JAMES: Yeah. That's why he painted 'em the way he had 'em painted those . . . colors.

CHRISTY: I was wondering about those . . . colors . . .

JAMES: Yeah. Joe's is the color Irene had in her head when she first saw him . . . and Irene's is the color Joe had in this head when he first saw her.

CHRISTY: Oh.

(Beat — looking at cars.)

JAMES: Honey — . . . Did you have a . . . color in your head when you first saw me?

CHRISTY: Um . . . *(She thinks.)* —

JAMES: I saw blue.

CHRISTY: Really?

JAMES: Yeah. First time I saw you, I saw blue . . . and I remember thinking that I had never seen blue like that before.

CHRISTY: I never knew that. I think I may have, too.

JAMES: Yeah?

CHRISTY: Seen blue.

JAMES: Yeah?

CHRISTY: Yeah

(Beat.)

CHRISTY: That was fun.

JAMES: Yeah.

CHRISTY: To remember.

JAMES: Yeah.

CHRISTY: What it was like when I first saw you.

JAMES: Yeah.

CHRISTY: I had almost forgotten.

JAMES: Yeah.

CHRISTY: Because now I just see . . . faded.

JAMES: Me too . . .

(Beat.)

JAMES: That's neat that they did that.

CHRISTY: Yeah.

JAMES: We should paint somethin' blue

    . . . somewhere

        . . . to remember.

CHRISTY: We should, yeah.

(James starts to go.)

CHRISTY: Where are you going?

JAMES: I'm gonna go get some paint. When I get the lime. And the pizza, // so we can paint something blue around here. >

CHRISTY: Honey, I don't want pizza, I got salmon.

JAMES: 'Cause I really think I'm ready for things to feel like they used to feel.

CHRISTY: So am I.

JAMES: I'm ready for us to be more like *they* are.

CHRISTY: Yeah —

JAMES: 'Cause I'm tired of feelin' like it's hard to be neighbors with them!

CHRISTY: Why do you feel like it's hard to be neighbors with them? They're the best kind of neighbors a neighbor could have!

JAMES: I know — it's just — just . . . all that they have and all that they do — They make me feel like I'm slipping.

CHRISTY: Slipping?

JAMES: Yeah, I've been feeling like that for a while, like we're slipping, like we've slipped, like we're losing, like we've lost. At first I thought it was just that they're doing so well, but then I started to wonder — is that it? Is it that they're doing so well, or is it that we're slipping? And I think it's that we're slipping. We've slipped. We just don't have what we used to have, and we aren't what we used to be. We've lost something somewhere along the way, and we've gotta find what that was, and I think the only way for us to do that again is if we start taking little steps to get us back to where we were, like kissing each other and limin' the lawns and painting the house, and getting up and going out.

CHRISTY: I know, I know. And I did that today, James. I got up —

JAMES: I know. // You said.

CHRISTY: No — and went out.

JAMES: *(This stops him.)* What?

CHRISTY: I've been trying to tell you that since you came home. I went out today. Outside. Got up and went out.

JAMES: *(This stops him.)* You did?

CHRISTY: Yeah.

JAMES: Well — that's great! >

CHRISTY: No, it's not, really, James —

JAMES: Where'd you go? What did you do?!?

CHRISTY: I went to the SuperCenter.

>   *(Beat.)*

JAMES: What?

>   *(Beat.)*

CHRISTY: I went to the SuperCenter.

JAMES: Oh.

CHRISTY: If I had known, I could have gotten you lime for the lawn there, and some blue paint for the house, even the pizza, if I had known you needed those things, because they have everything there.

JAMES: Yeah, that's where I was gonna go . . .

CHRISTY: Of course.

JAMES: to get those things . . .

CHRISTY: Of course.

JAMES: 'cause they have everything there.

CHRISTY: I know.

JAMES: Almost everything.

CHRISTY: Yeah. *(Beat.)* That's why I went.

JAMES: Oh.

CHRISTY: To see what I could find.

JAMES: Yeah.

>   *(Little beat.)*

CHRISTY: 'Cause you know something? I felt like we were slipping, too.

JAMES: You did?

CHRISTY: Yeah, I mean, Irene, goes to the SuperCenter every day, every single day, I see her getting stuff and things for Joe and the kids — mostly for the kids — and we don't have any kids . . . and for *herself.* There's, so much a person could get for herself at the SuperCenter, stuff to make her feel like she used to feel, things to make her look like she used to look, and so I went there! Got things. And stuff. To make me look like I used to look, feel like I used to feel — do I look better?

JAMES: Yeah —

CHRISTY: I feel like I do!

JAMES: You do!

CHRISTY: I wanted to look better for you, so that maybe we could have a little fun tonight since we haven't in a while. Had fun. Not 'cause of you. It's me, I know, >

JAMES: Honey —

CHRISTY: It's me. I haven't been much fun.

JAMES: Honey — Shh . . . *(He tries to soothe her physically.)*

CHRISTY: *(Not letting him soothe her.)* I was just gonna go grocery shopping, but then I thought, No, I'll go to the SuperCenter. I can get groceries there after I get us the stuff and the things we need, 'cause I realized I was *starving*, but, you know, if you stock up at the SuperCenter, you'll never starve, speaking of which — you must really be hungry, after a long, hard day at work!

JAMES: Starving!

CHRISTY: Yeah! Me, too — , so, why don't I get started on dinner? >

JAMES: Honey — wait!

CHRISTY: I hope salmon's OK, I got salmon: >

JAMES: Wait, honey —

CHRISTY: there was a special at the SuperCenter on salmon, so I got a box of SuperCenter salmon filets, 24-count —

JAMES: *(Stopping her.)* Wait, wait, wait. Dinner can wait.

CHRISTY: No — You're starving. And so am I.

JAMES: Honey! You got up today!

CHRISTY: Yup.

JAMES: And went out!

CHRISTY: Yup.

JAMES: And that's great.

CHRISTY: James! Getting up and going out is not great.

JAMES: It is, it is! *(Hugging her.)*

CHRISTY: *(Trying not to take the hug.)* Don't, don't, don't. Don't do that.

JAMES: What?

CHRISTY: Don't —. You don't hug people for getting up and going out.

JAMES: But —

CHRISTY: People get up and go out, James. You don't be proud of a person for getting up and going out.

JAMES: Yes, you do! It's underrated! Getting up and going out. It's hard to get up and go out. It's hard out there. Shoppin'! Especially at the SuperCenter, that's hard work! There's so much stuff there, so much space, so much service, so many service professionals. A person could get lost in there inside all that.

CHRISTY: I know that. It's why I haven't gone there.

JAMES: Yeah. That's why it's kind of a big deal that you did.

CHRISTY: Yeah.

JAMES: Go there.

CHRISTY: Yeah, well, *(Little beat.)* it won't be happening again for a while, because it was a little too much for me, a little too big out there for me, >

JAMES: Of course, of course.

CHRISTY: that's why I was in bed when you came home, // needed a little lie-down >

JAMES: I'm sorry — I didn't think you had gotten up —

CHRISTY: Well, I *had,* I *did,* >

JAMES: I know —

CHRISTY: because I wanted to get something so I could make us a nice dinner, because I decided — . . . that today *(Going to the window.)* I'm ready to be like them again. A consumer. I'm ready to consume again. I mean, we've got a lotta square feet to fill. And I'm ready to fill it!

JAMES: Oh, honey!

CHRISTY: What?

JAMES: You're just acting like you used to act! And looking like you used to look when I loved you more than anything in the world.

CHRISTY: I am aren't I?

JAMES: Yeah!

CHRISTY: It's a new day, James!

(Kiss.)

END OF SCENE

Cyclone
Ron Fitzgerald

Dramatic
Erin and Mitch, probably late twenties to early thirties

> *Mitch and Erin live together in a trailer park. Mitch has been acting very strangely of late.*

> *(Mitch stands at the edge of the yard drinking a beer. A pile of empties sits nearby. Across the yard, a hamburger is on a plate near the Flamingo.)*
> *(Erin walks up behind him. He doesn't turn. She lights a cigarette.)*

ERIN: The drinking seems to be going well.

MITCH: Yeah, you just have to apply yourself.

> *(He finishes his beer, tosses the empty onto the pile. Stares.)*

ERIN: You having a moment here or something?

MITCH: I was going to play some ball. But I can't play ball. Because the fucking dog stole my ball.

ERIN: Where'd you go last night?

MITCH: I told you.

ERIN: You told me you went for a ride.

MITCH: So. I went for a ride.

ERIN: Where to?

MITCH: Nowhere.

ERIN: I talked to Martin.

MITCH: Why don't you just tell him you're not interested.

ERIN: I'm not.

MITCH: So just tell him that. He keeps hanging around.

ERIN: He comes in for coffee and donuts.

MITCH: Hanging around and making speeches.

ERIN: Martin was talking about this guy with a gun at some store. He asked me where you were last night.

MITCH: What'd you say?

ERIN: I said you were home.

MITCH: It's none of his fucking business.

ERIN: Do you have a gun?

MITCH: It wasn't me. OK? I didn't do anything in any store.

> I just . . . I couldn't sleep. So . . . so I . . . you know . . . drove around. Don't worry about it.

ERIN: But I do worry. I mean . . . I want to help you deal with all of this.

MITCH: I don't need your help dealing with anything.

> Last time I saw my dad . . . he was driving away. He didn't look back. He sure as hell didn't wave.

(Mitch lights a cigarette. Erin looks across the yard.)

ERIN: Is that a . . . a hamburger?

MITCH: Yeah.

ERIN: Why is it sitting in our yard?

MITCH: I set a trap for the dog.

ERIN: You did what?

MITCH: He pissed on my flamingo. He crapped in my yard. He stole my ball.

ERIN: You can't have that.

MITCH: That's what I'm saying. I'm going to nail the little bastard.

ERIN: With a hamburger.

MITCH: That's just the bait.

ERIN: It's on a bun.

MITCH: It's a hamburger.

ERIN: Yeah but it's for the dog. I don't think the dog needs a bun.

MITCH: It has to look natural.

ERIN: So the dog doesn't get suspicious.

MITCH: It's a very smart dog.

ERIN: How do you know?

MITCH: I've seen him in action.

(They watch the burger.)

ERIN: You think it'll work without fries and a Coke?

MITCH: He'll be back.

ERIN: So the dog . . . sees the burger . . . eats it . . . and . . . what? Freaks out 'cause he can't leave a tip?

MITCH: Poison.

ERIN: Poison?

MITCH: He stole my ball. He crapped in my yard. He pissed on my flamingo.

ERIN: That's crazy. You're not going to poison the dog.

MITCH: I got no choice.

ERIN: You wouldn't poison a dog. You wouldn't do that.

MITCH: At this point, it's kinda him or me.

ERIN: You're talking about a dog.

MITCH: No, I'm talking about principle. The violation of my fucking property.

ERIN: What violation? Some poop?

MITCH: He stole my ball.

ERIN: Where the hell did you get poison?

MITCH: Look around.

(Mitch opens another beer.)

ERIN: Might want to chew some gum before you go to work.

MITCH: I'm not going to work.

ERIN: You take off?

MITCH: Kind of. I quit.

ERIN: You . . . ? What are you talking about?

MITCH: I'm talking about how I quit my job.

ERIN: You . . . you . . . ? Why?

MITCH: Because it sucked shit.

ERIN: You just up and quit?

MITCH: I'm supposed to . . . *what?* . . . just keep on working there . . . so someday I can be a . . . a manager . . . or a supervisor . . . maybe even a foreman . . . some other kinda fucking asshole? Work sixty, seventy hours a week to get myself a . . . a promotion . . . a step up . . . and so then I'm not exactly *drowning* in the shit . . . I'm just wading in it . . . just like ankle deep. It's still shit. It's still going to be the same shit. Every day. I don't want my life to be the same shit every day.

ERIN: Fuck you. The same shit.

MITCH: I'm not talking about you.

ERIN: Why? You think I go skipping off to work every morning?

MITCH: No.

ERIN: Spend my day picking bugs out of the icing . . . come home and I'm just . . . I'm just . . . the same old shit.

MITCH: I . . . I don't mean you . . . I don't mean you and me . . . I mean the, the . . .

ERIN: The *what?*

MITCH: I don't know!

ERIN: Your life can be whatever you want it to be.

MITCH: Right.

ERIN: It can.

MITCH: I'm sure that's true.

ERIN: It's true if you think it's true.

MITCH: Yeah.

ERIN: Do you think it's true?

MITCH: Sure. Why not.

ERIN: Do you? Really? I'm serious.
  (Pause.)

MITCH: I can get another job.

ERIN: I know that.

MITCH: They're always hiring somebody to do something.

ERIN: Yeah, but what do you want to do?

MITCH: I don't know.

ERIN: I mean, if you could do anything in the world . . . anything you wanted . . . what would you do?

MITCH: Anything?

ERIN: Yeah.

MITCH: I think I would be somebody else.

ERIN: Like who?

MITCH: I don't know. Somebody different.

ERIN: Different how?

MITCH: I don't know. Somebody who . . . who could . . . who was . . . I don't fucking know. What do you want me to be?

ERIN: I don't want you to be anything. I want you to be you.

MITCH: Well . . . that's what I am.

  So I guess we're all happy now.
  (Pause.)
  (He finishes his beer, crushes the can, drops it in the pile.)

ERIN: I have to go back.

MITCH: Yeah.

ERIN: I just wanted to catch you before you . . . went to work.

MITCH: Well. You caught me.

ERIN: Yeah.

(Mitch opens another beer.)

Have fun killing the dog.

(Erin walks off.)

(Mitch watches her go. He sips his beer, looks around the yard. He slowly walks over to the burger. Picks it up. Sniffs it. Takes a bite. Chews.)

END OF SCENE

Edna Discovers That One Thing About Herself That Makes All the Difference

Randy Wyatt

Dramatic
Man and woman, each in their thirties.

A typical breakfast at home.

WOMAN: I'm about ready for this to be over.

MAN: What? Breakfast?

WOMAN: No. This . . . uh, this . . . uh . . .

MAN: Relationship?

WOMAN: Exactly. This relationship. I'm pretty much done with it. I mean, why are we doing this?

MAN: A marriage needs a relationship. Somebody said so.

WOMAN: Who?

MAN: A bachelor, I bet.

WOMAN: A marriage, indeed. Why on earth did we ever get married?

MAN: It was your idea.

WOMAN: It was not. You proposed.

MAN: I was bored.

WOMAN: You're always bored.

MAN: Yes, I am. It conserves energy.

WOMAN: Maybe I'm bored too.

MAN: So take off. Pass the butter.

WOMAN: *(Passing the butter.)* Are you throwing me out of the house?

MAN: All I'm saying is . . .

WOMAN: Are you throwing me out of the house?!

MAN: *(Wearily, deadpan.)* Yes, I am. You and all your belongings. Pack. You have five minutes.

WOMAN: I can't believe you're saying this to me. I can't believe it's come to this. I can't believe it. It's unbelievable.

MAN: I only keep you around because the vacuum cleaner looks so idle at the breakfast table.

WOMAN: I . . . I am so . . . I don't know what I'm . . . going to do . . .

MAN: I do. You'll call Carolyn.

WOMAN: I am so sick of you telling me what I am going to do.

(Man hands her the cordless, which she dials without skipping a beat.)

WOMAN: *(Continuing.)* You can't possibly know what I am going to do next. I am not your puppet. I am not predictable. One of these days I will . . . Carolyn? It's me. Well, he threw me out of the house. Yes, just now.

MAN: Ask her if she wants to come over.

WOMAN: Well, I guess I'll just have to learn how to make it on my own, I suppose, not that that will be easy for a woman of my age. Uh-huh. Yes, I know, it's tragic.

MAN: Salt.

WOMAN: *(Passing the salt.)* It's atrocious, the way he treats me. Now he wants to know if you want to come over. No, Carolyn, not really. He's being ironic.

MAN: I am not. Ask her if she wants breakfast.

WOMAN: My God, he's making passes at you while I sit here, upon my life and soul. Well, he just said he wants you to come over for breakfast.

MAN: Yep, might as well marry her. She likes breakfast, I like breakfast, it's destiny.

WOMAN: I am speechless. Do you know what he just . . . yes, Carolyn, I know you like breakfast — How. Dare. You.

MAN: Is she taking me up on it?

WOMAN: Carolyn, it is . . . DISGUSTING . . . shameful . . . you picking up my man the instant he dumps me. What sort of friend are you?

MAN: Come off it, Edna, she's just hungry.

WOMAN: You know what this makes us? You know what this makes — I'll tell you what this makes us, Carolyn. Rivals. That's what that makes us.

MAN: Oh, good for you, dear, what you've always wanted. Here's the salt back.

WOMAN: *(Taking the salt.)* I am sure that you find this amusing, Carolyn, but I am not the type of woman who takes affronts such as these lying down. I may be a suburban housewife with a meek and humble nature, but I swear as God as my witness, you shall pay for your backstabbing lusts — both of you.

MAN: I bet she knows how to make an omelet. What the hell is this anyway?

WOMAN: Abuse. Abuse on the phone, abuse in my house. I'm trapped. Trapped like a hamster in a cage.

MAN: You're not supposed to cook it until it crunches. Spaghetti, brownies, omelets, none of it should be crunchy.

WOMAN: I'll tell you what I'm going to "do about it" Carolyn, I'm going to go over there right now and . . . and . . .

MAN: *(Helping her.)* Bust your ass up.

WOMAN: And bust your ass up! No, you heard me! I am not to be trifled with! I am a cauldron of boiling rage! I will be over there in fifteen minutes to bust your ass up as properly as I can muster! As soon as I am done with breakfast, mark my words.

MAN: Well done, dear. Very urban.

WOMAN: Are you . . . are you LAUGHING at me? You are an . . . *(Shouting into the phone.)* ASS!
(She hangs up violently.)

WOMAN: *(Continuing.)* What a woman.

MAN: Pepper.
(She hands the pepper out to him, but she is thoughtful, and does not let go of the pepper shaker when he reaches for it. This forces him to look at her.)

WOMAN: *(An epiphany.)* People don't take me seriously, do they?
(He looks at her with surprise. Lights down.)

END OF SCENE

Either/Or
Dan O'Brien

Dramatic
Dashiel and Magdalena, twenties to thirties

A couple are having it out about their relationship.

(Mid-morning on a Sunday. Coffee shop.)

MAGDALENA: I'm sorry

DASHIEL: No I'm sorry

MAGDALENA: It wasn't your fault

DASHIEL: It wasn't anybody's fault

       It just happened.

       Things like this happen.

       It happens: that's life.

MAGDALENA: It's not like I didn't like it.

       I liked it, you know, did you?

DASHIEL: I loved it.

MAGDALENA: — You did? You loved it?

DASHIEL: Well I always love it.

       Don't you?

MAGDALENA: Wow.

       I didn't know you loved it.

DASHIEL: Don't you?

MAGDALENA: Sometimes I love it.

       Sometimes I tolerate it.

DASHIEL: Well, you know, that kind of hurts my feelings.

MAGDALENA: It wasn't meant to hurt your feelings, Dashiel.

       "Dash."

       If it hurt your feelings it has more to do with it being the truth.

       You do want the truth, don't you?

DASHIEL: Do you?

MAGDALENA: Of course!

DASHIEL: I feel like when we see each other, "Magdalena" . . .

MAGDALENA: Yes? what?

DASHIEL: If we don't, you know, you feel unattractive.

MAGDALENA: Well I do feel unattractive.

> Now that you mention it:
> I feel fat.

DASHIEL: — And how do you suppose that makes me feel?

MAGDALENA: How does that make you feel?

DASHIEL: How can I feel attracted to someone who doesn't feel attractive?

MAGDALENA: You're not feeling attracted to me?

DASHIEL: I'm not feeling anything to you right now.

> We're talking about how you feel.

MAGDALENA: You don't feel attracted to me.

DASHIEL: That's not what I said.

> If you listen to me you'll realize what I say.
>
> You make me say things I'm not actually saying.

MAGDALENA: Have you ever thought that maybe the reason you don't feel attracted to me has more to do with the fact that you don't find me attractive anymore?

DASHIEL: No, that's not it.

MAGDALENA: Then what?

DASHIEL: You could let loose.

MAGDALENA: What?

DASHIEL: You could let loose.

> More.

MAGDALENA: I let loose. All the time.

DASHIEL: You used to let loose.

> You used to love letting loose.
>
> I used to love that about you.
>
> You were the first woman I knew who could let loose in that
way.
>
> In that way, it made you sort of a man.

MAGDALENA: What does that mean?

DASHIEL: It doesn't mean anything.

MAGDALENA: — What the fuck does that mean?

DASHIEL: It doesn't mean.

It means.

Look:

it means exactly what it means.

OK?

Everything doesn't have to mean something.

MAGDALENA: Well it actually does.

DASHIEL: That sort of thinking is, I think, a sickness.

MAGDALENA: — You're right: I don't love it.

DASHIEL: What?

MAGDALENA: I don't love it anymore.

I was speaking before out of habit or I don't know "politeness."

when I said I tolerated it.

I don't even tolerate it anymore.

I fucking hate it.

DASHIEL: I see.

What.

Am I doing something wrong?

MAGDALENA: You're not the problem here, Dash.

DASHIEL: Oh, so do you think maybe you're the problem?

MAGDALENA: Could be. Could be me.

DASHIEL: And what is it exactly you don't like about it?

MAGDALENA: The way it feels.

DASHIEL: Well that's.

Jeez.

That makes me feel.

— That's wrong.

You should love how it feels, even if all else fails.

MAGDALENA: What else fails?

What's the all else that could possibly fail here?

DASHIEL: I don't know, our trust, our intimacy.

Our lines of communications.

MAGDALENA: God I love it when you talk like a woman.

DASHIEL: — OK, hey, they're just words!

MAGDALENA: They're abstract!

Everything's fucking abstract!

DASHIEL: If we're not abstract, how are we ever going to — !

How are we ever going to wrap our — !

How are we. I don't know.

MAGDALENA: We communicate.

We're communicating right now.

I mean.

I mean.

Yes:

people could communicate more.

That would be nice.

This whole fucking world could use a little more face-to-face.

But considering what you and I have to deal with here —

DASHIEL: What do we have to deal with?

MAGDALENA: All the obstacles to the

DASHIEL: What obstacles?

MAGDALENA: I wish that

I wish

DASHIEL: What?

MAGDALENA: I wish I had a baby.

I wish there was a World War.

"Dear Lord send us war in our time."

A Great Depression to live through — an economic one.

Something we all had to face — as a culture.

There would at least be something to focus on.

Something besides ourselves, which if you look closely enough isn't anything at all.

There isn't anything there.

I could be anyone here.

Had a few things been different in my life.

I could be anyone in the future.

I could be anyone in this room.

Either/or.

Take your pick. *(Beat.)*

What were we talking about?

Sex?

DASHIEL: Do you ever do it alone? I do it alone all the time. Too much. When I don't do it, I feel stronger — I feel, I don't know, moral. But

I keep doing it all the same, on a more or less daily basis. Last Tuesday I did it three times. In succession. When I was done I felt like a sucked orange. Something in me felt depleted. I don't mean depleted I mean dead. Suddenly I felt like I couldn't feel anything anymore, and it felt good. And then I began to cry. And I felt this feeling that there was somebody else there, and she had these arms like wings and she laid them out over my . . . *(Beat.)*

Forget it.

MAGDALENA: Keep going.

DASHIEL: You don't understand.

MAGDALENA: You were feeling lonely, and?

You were feeling, and?

DASHIEL: You can't understand.

MAGDALENA: You were, and?

(Beat.)

You know what I think? I think we need to get to know each other, all over again.

(Beat.)

DASHIEL: All right.

You're right.

Let's not talk anymore.

(She gives him her hand.)

(A long pause here.)

MAGDALENA: I'm sorry.

DASHIEL: No I'm sorry.

MAGDALENA: It's not your fault —

(Lights out.)

END OF SCENE

Fugitive Pieces
Caridad Svich

Dramatic
Troubled John and Downcast Mary, teens

> *Where the rails converge. Troubled John is eating a Red Vine licorice twist from a bag. Downcast Mary watches him. They have been traveling for miles across country. Downcast Mary has carved John's name on her forehead as a sign of affection.*

DOWNCAST: You're going to get sick if you keep eating like that.

TROUBLED: I like to eat.

DOWNCAST: You're going to get us killed.

TROUBLED: What'd I do?

DOWNCAST: You steal all the time. Stuff we don't even need. Wind-up ducks.

TROUBLED: I hadn't seen one in a while. Not since I was a kid.

DOWNCAST: Broke down in five minutes.

TROUBLED: Made in China.

DOWNCAST: Jacks, yo-yos, pencil sharpeners, rock candy.

TROUBLED: We made it through the Carolinas on rock candy.

DOWNCAST: And that fucking peanut brittle. Messed up your teeth.

TROUBLED: I'll get them fixed.

DOWNCAST: With what?

TROUBLED: I'll work for a bit. I can lift things.

DOWNCAST: You can't even sign your name.

TROUBLED: What the hell are you talking about?

DOWNCAST: I've seen you looking at the signs on the road.

TROUBLED: 'Cause I couldn't read that billboard! Is that why — ?

DOWNCAST: Letters as big as me.

TROUBLED: I couldn't make sense of it, but I could read it.

> You're going to tell me you know what "Have Not. Will Go. Next Five Miles" means?

DOWNCAST: . . . You're a lousy thief.

TROUBLED: *(Indicating her forehead.)* Why'd you have to carve my name?

DOWNCAST: I thought you'd like it.

TROUBLED: It makes my lips itch.

DOWNCAST: Don't kiss me.

TROUBLED: Damn wish I could rub it out.

DOWNCAST: I could put a Band-Aid over it.

(He pulls another Red Vine out of the bag, eats.)

You're going to choke on that thing.

TROUBLED: You want one?

DOWNCAST: . . . You shouldn't steal.

TROUBLED: What?

DOWNCAST: It's wrong.

TROUBLED: You get me more morphine, all right? Crystal, powder, liquid . . . you get it.

DOWNCAST: It makes you retch.

TROUBLED: Ain' nobody caught us, have they?

Nobody's come round and picked us up for retching.

DOWNCAST: God looks down.

TROUBLED: Yeah? And what does He see? Fucking bird-claw man, Providence by the side of the road . . .

DOWNCAST: That was the devil's doing.

TROUBLED: You've got religion bad, don't you?

DOWNCAST: Some things aren't right. You spend your life making yourself think they are, but they're not.

TROUBLED: Like stealing?

DOWNCAST: Yeah. Or wishing ill on people, wanting them dead, beating someone up for a loaf of bread.

TROUBLED: You beat that guy — ?

DOWNCAST: On the train. Yeah. He wouldn't give it to me. I had to beat him up. I stuffed his handkerchief in his mouth, so he wouldn't say anything.

TROUBLED: You choked him?

DOWNCAST: He turned purple, that's all.

You think I'm going to let somebody die on me, give cops a reason to throw me under lock?

TROUBLED: Cops?

DOWNCAST: God looks down, John. He looks down. Wind-up ducks, yo-yos, ain't worth crap. You can't go into every dime-store on the road and walk out with a bag top-full of —

TROUBLED: What do you want me to do?

DOWNCAST: When I dropped down river, and ended up living on cigarettes

from the tail-end of Ohio straight through Kentucky and into Virginia,

I thought I'd die my lungs were so burned up.

Thought I'd end up stretched out on a long white table somewhere

with my new clothes on, and there wouldn't be a soul who'd weep for me,

'cause who'd know I was there? My folks in Kansas?

I was handed down to an aunt who handed me down to a cousin

who handed me down to a complete stranger who didn't know what to do with me.

"Go to the movies," he'd say, when he knew there wasn't a single movie theater in town,

"Leave me be."

I would hit the back wall of the house so hard the whole house would shake.

The stranger would come round and strap me with this long belt he had and say to me,

"You got to be put somewhere."

And he'd throw me down on the linoleum, turn on the gas, and shut the kitchen door

tight. And I'd dream of fire, with the end-buckle digging into my skin.

I'd suck air through my mouth. Slowly. And I'd breathe.

And when he got tired of listening to me breathe,

he'd open the door quietly and un-strap me.

So, there's no one, you see?

If I'm on a long white table, there's no one who's going to weep for me, except God.

And I thought to myself "I've been fooling myself against God.
I've twisted the whole world around

'cause of one stranger and a King Runt, and that ain't right."

And just as I'm thinking this, this old woman comes up to me.

She's got a wiry face and a parched blue dress, and she says

"Child, you need some milk. I can see your bones breaking from
here."

She starts to unbutton her dress.

Her breasts are young, bursting with milk.

And in the middle of a town square

With my lungs filled with nicotine

and my head spinning with memory,

I drink from her. I take her milk.

And when I'm done, she puts her hand on my forehead,

right across your name, and she smiles.

I think "I don't know what the Bible says.

But I know this: What this old woman has done is pure grace."

I'd never felt that.

TROUBLED: So, you want me to stop stealing 'cause some bitch comes up
to you and offers you tit?

DOWNCAST: You haven't prayed but once. Not since we left Virginia.

TROUBLED: Why should I pray? 'Cause some kick-ass strapped you up?

Go on. Step out on that rail with your fists clenched, Downcast.

DOWNCAST: Quiet.

TROUBLED: Hit me, Mary. That's what you're good at.

*(Downcast Mary slaps Troubled John. He slaps her back. She slaps him
again. Beat. Troubled John slaps her. She touches her face. She slaps him
again. He looks away. Beat. She touches her forehead, clenches her fists.
She moves a few paces to the left. She tackles him to the ground. They
wrestle for some time. Beat. Troubled John rises. From the ground, she
grabs his ankle. He walks, dragging her, five steps to the left. He stops.
Downcast Mary rises. She smooths her clothes. He coughs slightly. She
touches her forehead. He looks at her, smiles. Downcast Mary moves toward him. One step. Troubled John collapses. She looks out. Lights fade.)*

In Between
R. N. Sandberg

Dramatic
B and Cue, both in their teens

> *B has just overheard a conversation between Cue and Tad, leader
> of the popular crowd who bullies B. Cue and Tad were having fun
> mocking how B dances ("Doo, doo, doo, doo.") B gets up his courage
> to confront Cue as Tad runs off to attack a kid who's provoked him.*

CUE: *He's gonna kill that kid.*
    (There's yelling off stage — "Fight! Fight! Fight!" B moves closer to Cue.)
CUE: *Man, he's nuts. (She notices B.) Oh, hi. Aren't you gonna watch the
    fight?*

B: *I've seen Tad in action before. Him and his father.*

CUE: *Guys are so dumb.*

B: *Yeah, that's what I've always thought.*

CUE: *I didn't mean you.*

B: *You don't even know me.*

CUE: *You're right.*

B: Ya know what I do for fun? I collect insects. Bees and wasps and stuff.
    Shoot 'em off trees with my father's gun.

CUE: You're weird.

B: Yeah. I know you think that. Doo, doo, doo, doo.

CUE: Oh, hey, come on. I didn't mean —

B: Right.

CUE: *I didn't. We were just goofin' around.*

B: *Yeah, and I'm the joke.*

CUE: *No, wait. B, wait. Wait! I'm sorry. I shouldn't have done it. But you
    know how it is when you're messin' around. You just say stuff sometimes.
    If I'd known you were there — I was wrong. I apologize. Look, umm,
    look — there's this uh dance on Friday?*

B: *So?*

CUE: *Well, I know you probably don't usually go.*

B: *I go sometimes. With guys on the team.*

CUE: *Oh. Huh. That's good. Then, maybe, I'll see ya there.*

B: *You wanna see me at the dance?*

CUE: *Yeah.*

B: Oh, I get it. You and Tad and the crew wanna watch me. I'm a good show.

CUE: No. No. Not at all. I just thought — I don't know — maybe we could hang out or dance or something. I don't know, whatever. It could be a good time.

B: Yeah?

CUE: Yeah.

(Pause.)

B: *I uh don't shoot insects.*

CUE: I figured.

B: *I do stuff like anybody else.*

CUE: *Like runnin'.*

B: *Yeah. Sports, video games, stuff like that.*

CUE: *Sure.*

B: *It's funny. Runnin' and video games? They're a lot more alike than people think.*

CUE: *Yeah?*

B: *Yeah, when you're doin' well, you just sorta get in a zone and go with it.*

CUE: Huh.

B: *You ever play Halo?*

CUE: Uh uh.

B: You should. You'd like it. There's a city and it's the only habitable place on earth? And aliens every once in a while appear and you gotta blow 'em up? With guns and stuff, bazookas, rocket launchers? But there's a whole other part of it, too. You get to research and capture UFOs and go back into the alien world. That's the object of the game, to learn more about their world. I don't know what you're supposed to do with their world, but I'm tryin' to learn. I like learnin' about new stuff. Well — see ya, I guess.

CUE: Hey?

B: Yeah?

CUE: Your shirt? *(B tenses, anticipating a putdown.)* Nice color.

B: Cool. Yours too.

CUE: Cool.

B: Cool. See ya.

CUE: *At the dance, maybe, huh?*

B: *Yeah, maybe. (B saunters away. When he's almost off—) Yes! (He's gone.)*

CUE: *(To the audience.)* In my old school, there was a kid like him. James. His locker was next to mine. He was from Austria or Australia or somewhere. One day, he just kinda went crazy. Some guys were dissin' him and he jumped on one and started screamin'? The guys tore him off and stomped him. He never came back to school. I always felt bad. I mean, he was right next to me every day, and I never even talked to him. Maybe if I had, he wouldn't have snapped. When I see B, it brings that all back.

END OF SCENE

Indoor/Outdoor
Kenny Finkle

Seriocomic
Samantha, twenties; Shuman, twenties to thirties

> *Samantha and Shuman are having something of a couples-therapy
> session conducted by a woman named Matilda. Samantha is actu-
> ally a cat, and Shuman is her owner. Matilda, able to talk "cat,"
> has taught Shuman how to do it, too, so now he can communicate
> with Samantha, and she with him. They are in the midst of an ex-
> ercise Matilda has suggested.*

SHUMAN: I feel like I'm not enough.

SAMANTHA: I feel like I'm too much.

SHUMAN: I feel like no matter what I do you're not happy.

SAMANTHA: I feel like you never listen to me.

SHUMAN: I feel like I try to.

SAMANTHA: I feel like you do sometimes.

SHUMAN: I feel like sometimes I don't want to.

SAMANTHA: I feel like you're being honest.

SHUMAN: I feel like sometimes I get afraid.

SAMANTHA: I feel like sometimes I want more than you could give.

SHUMAN: I feel like I want to give you everything but don't know
how to.

SAMANTHA: I feel like I want to give some things to myself.

SHUMAN: I feel like I never knew that.

SAMANTHA: I feel like I need to be known.

SHUMAN: I feel like I want to know you.

SAMANTHA: I feel like you can't ever know me.

SHUMAN: I feel like I'd like to try.

SAMANTHA: I feel like it's too late.

SHUMAN: I feel like you're wrong.

SAMANTHA: I feel like you're wrong.

SHUMAN: I feel like you're being stubborn.

SAMANTHA: I feel like you're not listening to me.

SHUMAN: I feel like you're not letting me in.

SAMANTHA: I feel like you want to smother me.

SHUMAN: I feel like I just want to hold you.

SAMANTHA: I feel like I don't want to be held.

SHUMAN: I feel like you're afraid.

SAMANTHA: I feel like you're wrong.

SHUMAN: I feel like you want something from me I can't give you.

SAMANTHA: I feel like you could give it to me if you wanted.

SHUMAN: I feel like you want me to let you leave.

SAMANTHA: I do.

SHUMAN: I won't do that.

SAMANTHA: But that's what I want.

SHUMAN: I don't think you know what you want.

SAMANTHA: I don't think you know me well enough to know.

SHUMAN: I feel like we have a history together.

SAMANTHA: I feel like you want to live in the past.

SHUMAN: I feel like you want to live in the future.

SAMANTHA: I want to live with Oscar.

SHUMAN: I want to live with you.

SAMANTHA: I feel like Oscar knows me.

SHUMAN: I feel like I know you.

SAMANTHA: I feel like if you did, you wouldn't have thrown my mouse away!

SHUMAN: Your mouse?

SAMANTHA: Yes my mouse! I killed that!

SHUMAN: I know you killed it. It was going to start smelling so I threw it away.

SAMANTHA: It was mine.

SHUMAN: It was dead!

SAMANTHA: I loved that I killed that mouse and if you knew me at all you would have known that.

SHUMAN: How could I have possibly known that?

SAMANTHA: I told you.

SHUMAN: I feel like you didn't.

SAMANTHA: I feel like you weren't listening.
SHUMAN: I feel like you didn't try hard enough.
SAMANTHA: I feel like I did.
SHUMAN: Did you?
SAMANTHA: I did.

END OF SCENE

Indoor/Outdoor
Kenny Finkle

Seriocomic
Oscar and Samantha, both twenties

> *Samantha is a house cat, in love with Oscar, an alley cat, with whom she has run away.*

(Samantha and Oscar come running out.)
SAMANTHA: We did it! We did it!
OSCAR: I did it! I did it!
BOTH: WE did it!
SAMANTHA: Wow! Will you look at it out here?
OSCAR: Yeah. Home sweet home!
SAMANTHA: It's so . . . wild!
OSCAR: So let me give you a quick tour . . . This is fresh air.
SAMANTHA: *(Breathing in.)* Hello air.
OSCAR: This is grass.
SAMANTHA: Hello grass.
OSCAR: And these are trees.
SAMANTHA: Hello trees.
OSCAR: And up there are clouds.
SAMANTHA: HELLO CLOUDS!!!!!!
OSCAR: And past the clouds is the sun.
SAMANTHA: HELLO SUN!!!!!
OSCAR: And down that way is a river.
SAMANTHA: Hello, river!
OSCAR: And I'm Oscar.
SAMANTHA: Hello Oscar.
OSCAR: Hello Samantha . . . And this is Oscar feeling shy.
SAMANTHA: Hi shy Oscar.
> *(They stare at each other for a moment, awkwardly . . . and then . . . finally the two kiss.)*

SAMANTHA: I love you.

OSCAR: I love you too.

(He starts to lead her off.)

OSCAR: Come on.

SAMANTHA: Where are you taking me?

OSCAR: To the beach.

SAMANTHA: To the beach!!!!

(Oscar heads off in front of Samantha. She starts to go and right before she's gone, turns to the audience.)

SAMANTHA: So that's what we did. We headed to the beach. And along the way we stopped all over — in the big cities, deserts, mountains, you name it, Oscar and I saw it. And loved it. Every minute of it. Every detail.

Think the Discovery Channel in 3-D.

And then finally we made it to the beach. During the day there were tons of people around but at night, just like Oscar had promised, it was all ours.

(Samantha sits on the sand looking out. Oscar enters.)

SAMANTHA: Where were you?

OSCAR: I couldn't decide where to dump! There's so much sand!

(Beat. The two stare out.)

OSCAR: Isn't this heaven?

SAMANTHA: Yeah.

(Beat.)

OSCAR: So I'm thinking that in a few days we should head out for Alaska. I hear it's almost all snow there. Sound good?

SAMANTHA: Oh. Well I —

OSCAR: You what?

SAMANTHA: Nothing. I just thought — never mind.

OSCAR: No. Tell me. What?

SAMANTHA: I just thought we were going to stay here.

OSCAR: At the beach?

SAMANTHA: Yeah. I thought we were going to make this our home.

OSCAR: What do you mean?

SAMANTHA: I mean, I thought we'd make a house here.

OSCAR: Like with walls?

SAMANTHA: Yeah wouldn't that be fantastic?

OSCAR: It sounds kind of . . . small to me.

SAMANTHA: It wouldn't have to be . . . We could make it as big as we want.

OSCAR: But the whole world is our home. What's bigger than that?

SAMANTHA: Well I don't mean as big as the world, I just mean some place that's just ours. Our own place in the world.

OSCAR: I don't think I want a house. Look, Samantha, I'm an alley cat, I roam, that's all I've ever done.

SAMANTHA: We could try.

OSCAR: I don't think I could settle. I'm not sure it's in my nature.

SAMANTHA: We don't have to stay there all the time but wouldn't it be nice to have a place to go to . . . to know it's there?

OSCAR: I don't want that. I want to be free. I want to live on the sun and the sky and ground and our love.

SAMANTHA: I want our love to make a home.

OSCAR: Our love is home enough for me.

SAMANTHA: I don't think it's enough for me.

(Beat.)

OSCAR: So.

SAMANTHA: So.

OSCAR: Where does that leave you and me?

SAMANTHA: Go to Alaska. Love Alaska!

OSCAR: But where will you be?

SAMANTHA: I don't know.

OSCAR: But how will I find you?

SAMANTHA: When you're ready, you just will. Oscar, I love you.

OSCAR: I love you too Samantha.

(The two kiss.)

OSCAR: See you soon sweetheart.

(Oscar exits.)

END OF SCENE

Modern Orthodox
Daniel Goldfarb

Comic
Hershel and Rachel, both in their twenties

> *Hershel, an orthodox Jewish guy, has been having a hard time get-*
> *ting a girlfriend. Here, he is on a first date with Rachel who, it turns*
> *out, is his dream girl — both kosher and hot-to-trot!*

> *(Split stage. Rachel Feinberger, short, large-breasted, with an Eastern*
> *European–looking face, sits at a table at a kosher restaurant. She sips*
> *her pink drink. Checks her watch. Hershel enters.)*

HERSHEL: Excuse me, um . . . Rachel Feinberger?

RACHEL: *Baruch hashem,* yes. Are you Hershel?

HERSHEL: I'm afraid I am. Sorry I'm late.

RACHEL: It's alright. *Nu,* is that a gun in your pocket or are you just happy
to see me?

HERSHEL: No, it's a gun. *(He shows her the gun, puts it on the table.)*

RACHEL: I hope you don't mind, I ordered a Fuzzy Navel while I waited.
They're absolutely delicious. Schnapps reminds me of my dad. And
shul. All the men, shooters at morning *minyon.* Do you want one?

HERSHEL: *Baruch hashem,* your breasts are enormous.

RACHEL: *Baruch hashem,* thank you.

HERSHEL: I've never seen anything like them, except for in pictures of my
ancestors in the old country. They're like missiles.

RACHEL: Yes.

HERSHEL: You're stunning.

RACHEL: I don't know what to say, except maybe you're right. Men constantly start with me. Last Christmas, I mean December twenty-fifth,
I went to the *Matzoh* Ball at Webster Hall. I swear, the Israelis there?
I felt like a big piece of *schnitzel.* It's a test I think. You should have
seen the waiter when I ordered the navel. The way he looked at me.

Undressed me with his eyes. Wrote my order on the pad as if he were caressing my thighs. I swear, I think I blushed.

HERSHEL: You're quite a catch.

RACHEL: I guess so. *Baruch ha'shem,* that cactus over there, it's so phallic. Don't you think?

HERSHEL: Ummm, I've never eaten here before.

RACHEL: For kosher *Nuevo Latino,* it doesn't get any better.

HERSHEL: What's good here?

RACHEL: What do *you* think?

HERSHEL: *(To Rachel.)* Wow. *(To menu.)* Wow! Rice and beans is twenty-eight dollars.

RACHEL: Yeah.

HERSHEL: These kosher restaurants.

RACHEL: I know. They rob you blind. The Italians have their Mafia. *Baruch hashem,* we have *mashkiachs.*

HERSHEL: What to you mean?

RACHEL: It's just basic extortion. The *mashkiach* comes and says your restaurant isn't *traif,* and you pay through the nose for it. If you don't . . . *(She slits her throat with her finger.)* There goes your business.

HERSHEL: You thought of that all by yourself?

RACHEL: *Ken.*

HERSHEL: That's quite a *keppy* you got there on your shoulders.

RACHEL: *Nu,* so what do you do?

HERSHEL: I'm in diamonds.

RACHEL: Really. *Baruch hashem,* you must make a good salary.

HERSHEL: *Baruch hashem,* I get by.

RACHEL: Modesty becomes you, Hershel.

HERSHEL: You?

RACHEL: Marketing. But I'm treading water. My boss is a woman and you know how women are. They're making cuts. I'm not competitive. I have no future there. I'm just biding my time before I start having babies.

HERSHEL: You want a big family.

RACHEL: Of course. It's a commandment. Don't you?

HERSHEL: Do I? Do I ever! How long have you been working?

RACHEL: A year. I finished my masters in '03.

HERSHEL: Your masters?

RACHEL: I don't know how I did it. I'm not very bright.

HERSHEL: Yeshiva U?

RACHEL: Columbia.

HERSHEL: Uhuh.

RACHEL: *K'na Hora,* do you see that, over by the kitchen? That man wiping his face with the napkin?

HERSHEL: Uhuh.

RACHEL: He's starting with me. *(Perhaps she glares at him.)*

HERSHEL: How can you tell?

RACHEL: Before that napkin nonsense, he licked his lips at me. *(Perhaps she glares at him again, this time mouthing "What?!")*

HERSHEL: Maybe it was just guacamole.

RACHEL: So naive. Borderline adorable. Trust me, Hershel. *(Perhaps she mouths "I'm with him," rolling her eyes derisively.)*

HERSHEL: You seem to know a lot about men.

RACHEL: Yes, that's my gift and my curse, I'm afraid. When it comes to everything else, I'm less than nothing.

HERSHEL: Don't say that. You may have meager gifts in the brains department, but that is what *hashem* has chosen for you. I, myself, am no rocket scientist. But I know what I feel. And I feel like tonight is a very important night for me.

RACHEL: You're smooth for a religious.

HERSHEL: Let's order some food. . . .

(Hershel and Rachel are eating off each other's plates, as well as their own.)

HERSHEL: I like you.

RACHEL: Hershel!

HERSHEL: What can I say, I act with my heart. I learned today, from a great scholar, that sometimes it is very important to act with your heart.

RACHEL: Rabbi Akiva, Rabbi Tarphon, Rabbi Jose?

HERSHEL: No. A lady doctor named Hannah.

RACHEL: Is she old and saggy?

HERSHEL: No. She's a vision of tremendous beauty.

RACHEL: I see.

HERSHEL: But she's got nothing on you.

RACHEL: Hershel, you make me blush.

HERSHEL: Maybe, after we finish, I can kiss you on the mouth.

RACHEL: *Chutzpah!* Are you sure you're religious?

HERSHEL: As sure as I am that somebody's gonna get kissed.

RACHEL: *Baruch hashem,* double *chutzpah.* You have such strength. So masculine for a Jew.

HERSHEL: I've been reevaluating. I spent the last week with my good friends, my closest friends in the world, two ersatz Jews engaged to be married and living with each other in sin.

RACHEL: *(Gasps.) Baruch hashem!*

HERSHEL: Took the words right out of my mouth.

RACHEL: I think your Yankees *yarmulke* is darling.

HERSHEL: They have taught me a lot. It is they who used modern technology to bring us together. It is they who have taken me in in my moment of crisis and given me faith and hope, too. I can't wait to see them walk down the aisle. What a wedding it will be. To a genuine true love wedding. To Hannah and Ben.

RACHEL: To Hannah and Ben. . . .

RACHEL: I was reading on the Web about a beautiful ritual for the wedding night.

HERSHEL: Modern woman.

RACHEL: Are you interested in marriage?

HERSHEL: Are you?

RACHEL: Of course. I'm dying to try sex.

HERSHEL: Rachel!

RACHEL: That just kind of slipped out.

HERSHEL: You're incorrigible.

RACHEL: Are you a virgin?

HERSHEL: What do you take me for, a *goy* teenager? Of course.

RACHEL: Do you masturbate?

HERSHEL: Such questions. What's gotten into you?

RACHEL: My whole life, men start with me, but I don't probe. Tonight I'm gonna probe.

HERSHEL: I see.

RACHEL: So *nu?*

HERSHEL: It is against Jewish law to spill one's seed in vain.

RACHEL: You're just gonna give me the party line. Clever.

HERSHEL: Let's talk about something else . . .

RACHEL: I do it.

HERSHEL: What do you mean?

RACHEL: I do it.

HERSHEL: But you're a woman!

RACHEL: I know. No seed to spill in vain! I can do it as much as I want.

HERSHEL: Women do it?

RACHEL: Hershel, you're all red.

HERSHEL: *Baruch hashem. (Hershel starts breathing heavily.)*

RACHEL: Are you alright, Hershel?

HERSHEL: Yes, I'm OK. But let's please change the topic. There's modern I can deal with. That was a little postmodern if you know what I mean.

RACHEL: OK.

HERSHEL: You mentioned something about the Web, and weddings?

RACHEL: Yes. I read about this wonderful ritual. I love ritual.

HERSHEL: Me too!

RACHEL: It gives everything so much meaning.

HERSHEL: I agree.

RACHEL: It just sounded incredibly simple and romantic and spiritual.

HERSHEL: *Baruch hashem,* so tell me.

RACHEL: The newlyweds go to the room, and say the *she'ma* over the bed.

HERSHEL: I love it.

RACHEL: Then they cover the windows with towels, the crack in the door, all sources of light so the room will be completely dark.

HERSHEL: Scary.

RACHEL: Then the bride gets into the bed and the groom goes to the light switch by the door. He turns off the light and they undress in total darkness.

HERSHEL: *Ennn!*

RACHEL: *Psh.*

HERSHEL: *Dai!*

RACHEL: *Nu?*

HERSHEL: *Sha!*

RACHEL: The bride puts her legs in the air. The groom goes to her. The bride helps the groom find where he can know her as it can be a little hard to find sometimes. The groom tells the bride she is pretty and then fulfills his *mitzvah*. And then the bride compliments the groom on how well he did and cooks him dinner.

HERSHEL: Rachel Feinberger.

RACHEL: Yes?

HERSHEL: Will you marry me?

RACHEL: Hersh! *(Blackout.)*

END OF SCENE

Monkey in the Middle
Brighde Mullins

Dramatic
Darlene, mid-thirties; Top, early forties

> *Darlene and Top are in a bar in California. Top is an ex-Marine.*
> *Here, Darlene confesses a past indiscretion — which eventually leads*
> *to a violent chain of events.*

DARLENE: Top, didn't you sleep with a lot of different women in Vietnam?

TOP: — No

DARLENE: Didn't you and your buddies go to brothels —

TOP: — No

DARLENE: And for five dollars —

TOP: — No

DARLENE: Didn't you

TOP: I did not deflower any twelve year olds

I did not smoke any dope

I did not step on or near a land mine to put myself out of commission.

I did not hold Villagers at gun-point

You are the one person I thought understood me —

DARLENE: I never asked that last thing, that thing about Villagers —

TOP: Why are you looking to pick a fight? Why does your mind wrap itself around these suspicions? So readily, Darlene. So readily.

DARLENE: I am just talking. I am just saying what comes to mind.

TOP: Where did you get your information?

DARLENE: It's just that I read this thing about Amerasian kids, and I started thinking — what if one of these kids came to America, sponsored by the local parish and met, you know, a half-sister met her half-brother

TOP: So?

DARLENE: You know

TOP: No I don't

DARLENE: Well they could have a deformed baby, from inbreeding —

TOP: Lots of things COULD happen

DARLENE: That's what I'm saying. And: I know that you're a big flirt.

TOP: What do you mean?

DARLENE: You flirt with everyone, old ladies, nuns, the waitress with the humpback over at the IHOP.

TOP: You know I'm just a gentleman, Darlene.

DARLENE: I know that men can't help. Themselves. Something you should know is that I am considered, I am still considered attractive. In some circles.

TOP: You think I don't know that. I see men look at you, you think I don't know what they're thinking —

DARLENE: There are alotta things You Don't Know.

TOP: Yeah. Tell me some.

DARLENE: Get me some garnishes.

TOP: Garnishes?

DARLENE: Ask the bartender if I can have one of those big fat martini olives.

TOP: Why don't you just order a martini?

DARLENE: I am trying to stop, you know. I have not had a drink, but still have the fortitude to accompany you to a bar.

TOP: I've heard this before. You gotta do things the Greek way, Darlene, Moderation. Like me; I have one or two beers, that's that, right?

DARLENE: Wrong. One, two, three . . . seven. So the thing is I am trying to be honest with you, tell you some things about me, some things you probably unconsciously already suspect, you have an intuition —

TOP: Keep going

DARLENE: Such as when you ask "Why is Tara so BIG?" and "How Come Timmy is so Heavy" and I say that they are Throwbacks, whereas Martin looks just like you.

TOP: Keep going

DARLENE: Do I need to?

TOP: You need to

DARLENE: Two plus two equals four, right?

TOP: One, two, three, seven; and now two plus two

DARLENE: I got lonely when you were on tour of duty — Why'd you have to do so many? I got lonely, that's all.

TOP: You're saying WHAT exactly. You fooled around when I was stationed in Da Nang? You're saying you were out on one of your benders, and you were listening to Patsy Cline and getting sad and you wanted to just be held — and so you went home with SOME TOTAL FUCKING STRANGER some jerk on the make and you thought it would be fine and cozy and safe and then he raped you, is that what you're saying? You're saying you were raped by some ANIMAL, right? And you're saying that you felt ashamed to tell me, 'cause after all you went to a bar in some fucking "fuck-me" outfit and then you even went home with some guy during which time MY ASS was on the line in a fucking rice paddy on the edge of a jungle —WHO WAS IT?

(Very long pause.)

DARLENE: That's all you can say?

TOP: WHO WAS IT?

DARLENE: This is why They said to talk in a public place, so it would remain a conversation —

TOP: Who was it?

DARLENE: I was so lonely. For you. It was not decent behavior, I know.

TOP: So *you* seduced *him.* Who was it?

DARLENE: This is not at all the way it went in Role Playing.

TOP: What do you expect? You got some Brain Housing Unit, Darlene

DARLENE: We've been together a long time!

 END OF SCENE

Natural Selection
Eric Coble

Comic
Henry and Suzie, mid-thirties

> *Suzie and Henry are a married couple living in the Computer Age
> gone over the top.*

SUZIE: Hi, hon. I didn't hear you pull up.

HENRY: Stealth. I'm working on my stealth driving.

> *(Presenting the flowers.)*

> Da, da-da-da-da-da DAAAA!

SUZIE: Henry, are these real?

HENRY: Yep. The garden crew made them. They just came out of the tube
yesterday.

SUZIE: They're gorgeous. Let me get a shot of them.

> *(She aims her little webcam at the flowers.)*

SUZIE: *(Continued.)* These are so much nicer than the synth ones we have
at work.

HENRY: And I bought us dinner! Lasagne burritos.

SUZIE: *(Kisses him.)* Ooo, Henry —

HENRY: I thought a little romantic meal before Terrance comes downstairs
from school —

SUZIE: He's actually up there in soccer practice right now. It's being
webcast in real time. I was checking in on it —

HENRY: *(Looks at her laptop screen.)* How's he doing?

SUZIE: Pretty well. The coach has been instant messaging notes on what
he needs to work on —

HENRY: We're so lucky we got Mr. Klerksdorp is willing to coach from
South Africa. I'm gonna download some more tips for Terrance to
send them to his friends.

SUZIE: I don't know when he's going to have time for that before the school
play though. Let me get a shot of you and the flowers.

(She points the webcam at Henry who poses.)

SUZIE: *(Continued.)* This is going straight onto my blog.

(Typing.)

SUZIE: *(Continued.)* "6:52 p.m. B-HOE brings flowers and dinner —"

HENRY: "B-HOE"?

SUZIE: "Best Husband on Earth." My acronym for you ever since you re-grouted the bathroom.

(She kisses him again as he opens his own laptop and sits down.)

HENRY: Man's gotta do what a man's gotta do.

SUZIE: Most of my readers all agree — the feedback is skewing highly in your favor. And this picture of you with the flowers is darling.

(Showing him her screen as she types.)

"Is there a more darling man?"

(To Henry.)

You got the burritos at Applebee's?

HENRY: Of course.

SUZIE: *(Typing.)* I'm hyper-linking to them. I'm sure they'll appreciate the plug.

HENRY: *(Looking at his screen.)* Huh.

SUZIE: What.

HENRY: Oh, I was just checking the weather.

SUZIE: Why? You're not going back out are you?

HENRY: No. Just looking at the southwest United States. Looks clear and dry. Good flying weather.

SUZIE: You're not re-tracing the butterfly migration patterns again, are you? You know they're not coming back, sweetheart.

HENRY: No. Ernie's flying out to Arizona, Utah, to look for new stock for the Native Pavilion.

SUZIE: I thought he was in the Adirondacks.

HENRY: That didn't work out.

SUZIE: Send a camera with him this time. I can post his shots in the "Can You Believe It" section of my site.

HENRY: That's a fantastic idea, honey.

SUZIE: Always thinking. You want your burrito heated up?

HENRY: Maybe I can go with him and shoot the photos myself.

(Suzie pauses.)

SUZIE: What?

HENRY: Since he's going anyway, I could tag along. E-mail some pictures back to you and the office —

SUZIE: You're not going to Utah.

HENRY: Maybe not Utah, but maybe Arizona and New Mexico.

SUZIE: Are you insane?

HENRY: I hardly think it's insane for a curator to go out and collect artifacts for his exhibits —

SUZIE: Are we talking pots or people?

HENRY: . . . both.

SUZIE: Forget it.

HENRY: But —

SUZIE: Uh-uh. No way. Ernie came to your office today, didn't he? You told him about the desert dream, didn't you —

HENRY: I didn't —

SUZIE: *(Typing.)* "6:54 p.m. Former B-HOE goes completely off his rocker —"

HENRY: Don't make me a Former B-HOE — I'm not a *former* B-HOE —

SUZIE: *(Turns the camera on herself and types.)* "If anyone's watching this in real-time — HELP! My husband's gone suicidal —"

HENRY: We need new natives — I'll just run to get some new natives —

SUZIE: Can't you just paint some interns brown?

HENRY: Suzie!

SUZIE: We're talking about the desert, right, Henry?

HENRY: Exactly — plateaus, cliff dwellings, painted sand —

SUZIE: — and how many miles to the nearest TGI-Fridays?

HENRY: I'm sure there's good restaurants in Santa Fe, Phoenix — I don't know —

SUZIE: Exactly. You don't know. How often have you left Orlando?

HENRY: I go to conferences all the time — Toronto, Berlin, Cairo —

SUZIE: Places where they speak English and have running water and cell phone reception. Not the desert. Not Wile E. Coyote country.

HENRY: I know.

SUZIE: *(Typing.)* I bet there's a Traveller's Advisory on the Southwest —

HENRY: Of course there's a Traveller's Advisory — there's Advisories about the entire planet —

SUZIE: *(Reading her screen.)* Sunlight at 730% Recommended Daily Allowance, Particulate Matter at 210% RDA, new viruses reported in thirteen counties, 56% chance of Separatist activity —

HENRY: I know.

SUZIE: I am *not* going to be a single mother widow to our son.

HENRY: I know —

SUZIE: On my income! Can you imagine? Wal-Mart pays well, Henry, but not that well.

HENRY: Suze —

SUZIE: You don't want to pull up the rug!

HENRY: What??

SUZIE: You said you'd pull up the carpet on the stairs to the attic this weekend — you're trying to get out of pulling up the carpet, aren't you!

HENRY: Oh God.

SUZIE: You're scared. You're scared of dust mites, aren't you?
(Typing.)
"Hubby'd rather face plagues and killers than pull carpet tacks —"

HENRY: Will you stop typing on your blog?? This is a private conversation —

SUZIE: My readers thrive on my private conversations — I keep it real, Henry, you will *not* edit me —

HENRY: And you won't edit me, Suzie!
(They stop. Staring at each other . . .)

HENRY: *(Continued.)* This isn't my idea. Yolanda's making me do it.

SUZIE: . . . oh God.

HENRY: My performance review is coming up, if I don't bring back something —

SUZIE: She's willing to kill you to restock the park!

HENRY: She's willing to risk me, not kill me, we don't know that I'll die —

SUZIE: I hate here. I hate her I hate her I hate her —

HENRY: I know. I guess it's my turn to look into the dread maw and say "Fuck You."
(Beat. He holds her.)

I can pull up the carpet tacks when I get back on Tuesday.
(Pause.)
SUZIE: What are you going to tell your son?
HENRY: I guess . . . I have to tell him I'm going on an adventure.

END OF SCENE

Never Tell
James Christy

Comic

Hoover, an opportunistic slacker, funny, deadpan, twenties; Liz, quiet, troubled, introverted, twenties

Hoover and Liz were recently set up for a double date by a mutual friend (Anne). It ended badly. Liz has been having anxiety attacks in which her mind blanks and she can't remember basic things.

(Liz is asleep on her couch, mumbling in her sleep. Hoover knocks at her door, she wakes up and answers it.)

HOOVER: Hey. How's it goin'.

LIZ: *(Groggily.)* Fine.

HOOVER: You look tired.

LIZ: I was asleep.

HOOVER: Yeah? That's cool.

LIZ: Yeah. It was.

HOOVER: *(Enters.)* I like your place.

LIZ: There's nothing in it.

HOOVER: You got milk crates, I like milk crates.

(Hoover starts going through the contents of one of her milk crates, and taking out CDs, videos, and books.)

LIZ: Yeah, milk crates are alright.

(She watches him rifle through her belongings, which he does throughout the scene.)

LIZ: Was there something you wanted?

HOOVER: Not really. Oh, I was going to apologize for the thing at dinner, I thought you might be mad or something.

LIZ: I'm not.

HOOVER: It seemed like you were mad me and Anne were talking about you behind your back. Like it bothered you.

LIZ: It didn't.

HOOVER: It seemed like it did.

LIZ: I'm telling you it didn't.

HOOVER: Why did you act like it did if it didn't?

LIZ: I don't know.

HOOVER: That's misleading.

LIZ: Are you a venture capitalist?

HOOVER: No.

LIZ: Then you were misleading.

HOOVER: No, I was lying. Big difference.

LIZ: Really?

HOOVER: Yeah. So why'd you mislead us?

LIZ: Because I wanted to leave.

HOOVER: Why'd you want to leave?

LIZ: I wanted to be alone.

HOOVER: That happen to you a lot? Where you're with people and you'd rather be alone.

LIZ: Sometimes.

HOOVER: So why'd you come back to New York? This place is crawling with people.

LIZ: I needed a change.

HOOVER: But you haven't unpacked.

LIZ: No, I haven't unpacked. Listen, I'm a little tired —

HOOVER: Has this always been true for you? This thing about people?

LIZ: Not really. Maybe a little.

HOOVER: You think it's why you have those panic attacks or whatever?

LIZ: I don't know. Listen, why do you care anyway? We don't really know each other.

HOOVER: That's it, I'm trying to get to know you better.

LIZ: Why?

HOOVER: Why not?

LIZ: I just don't see anything really coming out of it.

HOOVER: Oh, I think it will. I think something will come out of it.

LIZ: What?

HOOVER: You know how you said you needed a change?

LIZ: Yeah.

HOOVER: I'm the change.

LIZ: How are you the change?

HOOVER: I don't know how to say this.

LIZ: Just say it.

HOOVER: *(Exhales.)* You and I are going to spend the rest of our lives together.

(Beat.)

LIZ: Really?

HOOVER: Yeah.

LIZ: When did you decide this?

HOOVER: Today at work. But I didn't decide. I had this sort of vision. And
you were in it. You were all over it.

LIZ: I was. So what about me, do I have any choice in this?

HOOVER: Choice doesn't really enter into it. This is fate.

LIZ: Oh, it's fate. You didn't tell me it was fate.

HOOVER: It is.

LIZ: The rest of our lives? That's, that's a long time.

HOOVER: Yeah, tell me about it. I mean, I like my independence, you
know, I don't like to get tied down.

LIZ: *(Smiles incredulously.)* I'm tying you down?

HOOVER: No, well it's not your fault.

(Sees her look.)

I guess this is sort of out of nowhere for you after one date.

LIZ: I wouldn't even call it a date.

HOOVER: Well, whatever, after meeting once.

LIZ: For less than forty minutes.

HOOVER: Right. So it's a bit sudden. But the point is, it'll be a better thing
for you, us being together.

LIZ: A better thing?

HOOVER: I mean, I think there's something wrong. With you.

LIZ: This is how you pick up women? Does this work?

HOOVER: I'm just saying I think I could help. And these attacks, they won't
happen when you're with me.

LIZ: Why not?

HOOVER: Because you won't be scared anymore.

LIZ: *(Beat.)* Listen, I like you. I do. I don't understand what you want
and what the hell you're doing here, but I like you anyway.

HOOVER: What does it feel like?

LIZ: Let me finish. Now if Anne told you to come here to boost my spirits or something, you've done your job —

HOOVER: No one told me to come here. When you have a panic attack, how does it feel?

LIZ: I don't know. Not good.

HOOVER: How exactly. What happens.

LIZ: What difference does it make?

HOOVER: It'll make you feel better. Telling me.

LIZ: Will you leave?

HOOVER: Yes, then I'll leave.

LIZ: Fine.

(Beat.)

I'm presenting to an important client in this meeting, and mid-sentence I realize I can't remember his name. And the doubt spreads in my mind until I don't know anyone's name, my boss, my co-workers, I don't even know where I am. It's like your brain won't shut up.

HOOVER: So what did you do?

LIZ: I walked out.

HOOVER: And you never went back.

LIZ: right.

HOOVER: How do you feel now?

LIZ: Fine.

HOOVER: Didn't I tell you? I said you'd feel better after talking about it.

LIZ: I said "fine." I didn't say "better."

HOOVER: You seem better.

LIZ: I'm glad you think so.

HOOVER: I'm going to make you happy.

LIZ: How are you going to make me happy?

HOOVER: I'm going to make you think about good things instead of bad things.

LIZ: That's your help? Think about good things instead of bad things? You should be a therapist.

HOOVER: Therapy is for losers.

LIZ: I think we're done here.

HOOVER: I'm gone.

    (Not moving.)

    I really do like this place.

LIZ: Good. I'm going to go back to sleep now.

HOOVER: OK. You do that.

    (Liz grabs a pillow and lies down on the couch to resume her nap. Hoover resumes going through milk crates. Blackout.)

END OF SCENE

The Scene
Theresa Rebeck

Seriocomic
Charlie, mid-thirties; Clea, early twenties

> *Charlie is an out-of-work TV actor. He has met Clea at a party. He thinks she's an airhead — but on the other hand, she's incredibly sexy. Here, he has brought her back to his apartment for sex. At the end of this scene, Charlie's wife, Sheila, walks in on them.*

> *(Charlie's apartment. Clea and Charlie are having sex on the couch, and elsewhere. They are both in a half state of undress, as if they hit the ground running. It is quite athletic. After an extended and quite vocal climax, they collapse.)*

CLEA: Oh, God. Don't stop. No, don't stop. Don't stop!

CHARLIE: You got to give me a minute here, Clea.

CLEA: No, don't stop —

CHARLIE: How old did you say you were?

> *(He means it half as a joke, but it does stop her.)*

CLEA: No no don't do that. Don't categorize me.

CHARLIE: *(Still breathless.)* Asking you how old you are is categorizing?

CLEA: You're trying to define age as a life characteristic. As like, something that says something about a person.

CHARLIE: It does say, how old you are.

CLEA: No, it doesn't. It really doesn't. You say, "how old are you" like I'm young and you're old, like that's some joke, because you think you're old? But you're timeless. You're like this incredible lion who's been stalking the earth since the dawn of nature, or something.

CHARLIE: Tell me, do you actually believe all this crap that you keep spouting?

CLEA: Of course I believe it. Maybe you should try believing it, too. Why wouldn't you want to believe that you're a timeless lion? Isn't that better than thinking you're some old loser who can't get a job?

(She climbs on him and starts to kiss him. He pushes her away, sudden, stands and puts his pants on.)

CLEA: *(Continuing.)* No no. Don't do that. That's what I'm saying, that's not who you are!

CHARLIE: We have to get you out of here.

(He starts to dress, and straighten out the room again.)

CLEA: We just got here.

CHARLIE: And now we have to go.

CLEA: You said she was going to be at work, all afternoon, she's off screaming somewhere, come on, you said, we have all afternoon. Be a lion.

CHARLIE: I think we've had enough of the lion, Clea.

CLEA: I haven't. I mean it. I can go all day, and all night, I could go a whole weekend. Have you ever done that? Just, spent a whole weekend inside, doing things . . .

CHARLIE: Don't you get sore?

CLEA: You want to find out?

CHARLIE: Jesus! You're like, it's like talking to a porno movie —

CLEA: You are so hung up about the way I talk all the time!

CHARLIE: Well, it's very unusual, Clea, to find someone so remarkably uninhibited in so many ways —

CLEA: Yeah but you always turn it around, like you don't like it. You make it sound like it's maybe not so great, the way I am. That I'm sort of stupid, or just stupid or something —

CHARLIE: "Voracious" is actually the word I was thinking of.

CLEA: Yeah, like that's a bad thing. But you know what? You like it. It's actually driving you crazy how much you like it. Why can't you just say it? If I'm voracious then you're something that wants voracious more than anything it ever saw before.

CHARLIE: How can you know so much and so little at the same time?

CLEA: You have no idea, how much I know. Come on. We have all afternoon.

(She kisses him. He is increasingly a lost man. He tries to push her away.)

CHARLIE: We do have all afternoon. Just, not here.

CLEA: Ohhh please . . .

CHARLIE: Listen to me. This is my apartment.

CLEA: I know. I love it that you brought me here. It's so hostile.

CHARLIE: You are really something.

CLEA: Yes, I am. And you're the one who brought me here, to have sex in your apartment.

(Things are heating up again.)

CHARLIE: Stella could just walk in on us —

CLEA: *(Laughing.)* That would be hilarious.

CHARLIE: Yeah, no, it wouldn't.

(He pushes her away, firm. Looks at her, suddenly simple and clear and a little desperate.)

CHARLIE: *(Continuing.)* I mean, you understand what this is. We're clear on what this is, right?

CLEA: Relax. I know what this is. You're at a place, so am I. This is that place.

CHARLIE: Yes.

CLEA: It's what you need and I want, and that's why it's so hot. Trust me. I understand what this is.

CHARLIE: Good.

(Unsure, hoping that was clear, he leaves the room. She watches him go, goes to her purse, and takes out an apple, starts to eat, and calls to him in the next room.)

CLEA: *(Yelling.)* You know what we should do tonight? My friend can get me into this party. It's up on the upper West Wide so it is totally not like a really hip scene or anything, but there's going to be some movie stars there, she wouldn't tell me who, but they also have this hot tub there? On the roof. She went to a party at this place a couple weeks ago, and everyone takes their clothes off and gets in the hot tub. And then they have these cater waiters come around, I'm not kidding, with sushi. So you sit in the hot tub and like talk and eat sushi naked. It sounds so nineties, doesn't it?

Movie stars and sushi in a hot tub? Maybe they'll play R.E.M. on the "record player." Or do lines of cocaine. It's so unbelievably retro, a hot tub on the roof. I soo want to go.

CHARLIE: *(Entering.)* I've been to this party.

CLEA: Get out.

CHARLIE: I swear to God, I went to that party twenty years ago. Riverside Drive, ninety-six or seven and Riverside.

CLEA: I don't know.

CHARLIE: Sushi and cocaine in the hot tub on the roof? I went to that party. No kidding. I was doing this play Off-Broadway, completely unintelligible horse shit, and one of the other actors knew somebody who was going to this party, on the upper West Side. This rich guy, nobody knew his name, and the place is like a mansion, right, he owns the whole building and it's got art deco everything, completely tasteless. The place was huge, like five floors, people screwing in corners of the den and the living room, there was a three-way going on in one room, I'm not kidding, real hedonistic shit. And then there's that the hot tub up there on the roof with the greenhouse.

(Laughing now.)

He's got a fucking greenhouse up there, growing cactuses and hibiscus, something, I can't believe I remember this, everybody was completely coked out of their minds, like all night, till five, six in the morning. The nineties, that's how stupid we all were. It's amazing most of us are still alive. I was such hot shit. That play was terrible but it got inexplicably great reviews and I was . . . the world was on fire for me, boy. Sushi and cocaine and whatever I wanted. God that was fun. That was really fun.

CLEA: Well, guess what, it's your lucky night. Because you can go to that party again. With me.

CHARLIE: *(Reality check.)* I can't go to a party with you.

CLEA: Why not?

CHARLIE: Because I can't.

CLEA: It'll be realllly fun. That's what you said, it was reallly fun.

CHARLIE: I'm not going to a party with you, Clea!

CLEA: No one will see us! That's the whole point, that scene is completely over, so it won't matter!

CHARLIE: Great.

CLEA: You said yourself, the guy who owns this place is so nobody on Earth that is important, just some rich guy with a lot of money and a house with a hot tub, we can totally just go together. I mean, with my friend, we can dump her when we get there, which will be fine with her, she dumps me all the time.

CHARLIE: Look, I have — a life, Clea.

CLEA: Don't you mean, a "wife?"

CHARLIE: Yeah. That's what I mean. And like you said that scene is over. I'm not going to a party with you.

(He continues straightening the apartment.)

CLEA: No, come on, forget about her! You should see how much happier you are when you forget about her. We don't have to go to any party. Let's just pretend we're at a party. We're in the hot tub right now. No. No. Let's skip the hot tub.

I like the sound of those rooms, where people are just doing things, in the middle of somebody's house, who they don't even know whose house it is. Let's just think about doing it in front of everybody, in somebody else's room . . . .

(She reaches up and kisses him. He kisses her back.)

END OF SCENE

The Scene
Theresa Rebeck

Seriocomic
Charlie and Stella, mid-thirties

> *Stella has just come home early from her job as a booker on a TV*
> *talk show to find her husband, Charlie, having sex with an incredibly*
> *sexy younger woman named Clea.*

STELLA: Why?

CHARLIE: Don't ask why.

STELLA: *(Suddenly furious.)* Don't ask — why? "Why" is off the table? You
just completely — that was the most humiliating — I'm humiliated,
Charlie! I'm, I'm everything is, my whole life is suddenly not
even — and for *that?* And I'm not allowed to ask WHY?

CHARLIE: This is just, I can't — I can't . . .

STELLA: Stop being such a fucking coward and say something!

CHARLIE: You're too competent.

(There is a silence at this.)

STELLA: What?

CHARLIE: Everything. Gets done. Even when you hate what you're doing,
you get it done. You're like a machine. Everything gets done.

STELLA: *(Almost in tears, suddenly.)* I'm not like a machine. That's a lie.

CHARLIE: You're coherent. Everything coheres, and I, I can't — anymore — because I'm — and you're perfect. Your feelings are perfect.
Your work is perfect. You hold down a job you think is stupid and
it frustrates you in the perfect way. Even in how you're *not* perfect,
even in how things get to you, you're just, even your neurosis is perfect. You're so fucking competent, you don't ever expect too much
out of life. You handle all of it. Even this. Even this! I'm watching
you — you're handling it. You're already going to forgive this. THAT
WAS A FOREGONE CONCLUSION. And then I'll have that, too.

Your competence, and your forgiveness. Oh and your money, let's not forget that.

STELLA: So this is my fault?

CHARLIE: *(Snarling.)* No! It's my fault! It's my crime! And I own it! It's the only thing you left me, the ability to fuck up, and I want it! It's mine! This fucking disaster is mine, and you can just keep your fucking hands off of it!

STELLA: I don't understand why this is happening. Why are you talking to me like this?

CHARLIE: I'm talking to you like this because this is who I am! And I'm sick of pretending to be perfect, like you, because that is not the person I want to be!

STELLA: This is some sort of fucking midlife crisis. You want to fuck idiotic twenty somethings because that's what everybody else does, there isn't even a shred of originality in this —

CHARLIE: I wasn't looking for originality, Stella. I was looking to feel like someone who still had a shred of life in him!

STELLA: And fucking great-looking idiots is the only way you can do that? Are you kidding me? I mean it. You don't like your life so you honestly think that screwing that girl — that girl who can hardly speak — who has no character or substance or anything — that that is going to do something, for you, make you whole, make you understand who you are in the world —

CHARLIE: I don't want that. Don't you understand?

STELLA: This is just, it's just self-loathing, Charlie! You're projecting your self-loathing all over the rest of us and destroying everything so you can destroy yourself —

CHARLIE: Thanks, Stell, that's really, this is a thrilling moment to be psychoanalyzed —

STELLA: What else am I supposed to do?

CHARLIE: Nothing! Don't do anything! And don't explain this because I don't want to understand it! I just want to feel something. Remember when you felt things?

STELLA: I feel things!

CHARLIE: You feel unhappy. You feel competent. You feel like a wall.

STELLA: Don't you tell me what I feel. I feel disgust!

CHARLIE: You know what? She's right about one thing. If you want me to stay, you really don't know the first thing about how to make that happen.

(He heads for the door.)

STELLA: Where are you going?

CHARLIE: I'm going to a party.

(He slams the door. Blackout.)

END OF SCENE

The Search for Cindy
Tim Kochenderfer

Dramatic
Tim, late twenties; Cindy, mid-twenties

> *Tim has just had his girlfriend Cindy's name tattooed on his back.*

> *(Tim's house. Tim admires the tattoo on his back in the mirror. It is a giant heart with the name "Cindy" inside, with an arrow in the heart. The doorbell rings. Tim quickly puts his shirt on and opens the door. Cindy walks in.)*

TIM: Cindy, I was just about to head over to your house.

CINDY: Tim, we need to talk.

TIM: *(Pause, confused:)* Yes . . . Yes of course. We shouldn't just sit here, um, silently.

CINDY: No, I mean we need to talk about stuff.

TIM: *(Pause, still confused:)* Yes, I'm sure we'll think of some subjects.

CINDY: No, I mean we need to talk about us.

TIM: Good, because I have a surprise that has to do with us.

CINDY: No, Tim, listen, I'm bracing you, OK? I'm bracing you right now for something.

TIM: *(Oblivious.)* OK, well it sounds like you've got some really good news, so go ahead.

CINDY: First, I think we should break up and this next part isn't so easy for me. That necklace you got me for Christmas, I had to take it back to get refitted. *(Pause.)* Wait, I think I got those backwards.

TIM: What?! What are you talking about?

CINDY: What, about the break, up, the necklace or my sentence structure?

TIM: The break up!

CINDY: Yes, that. I think we should break up. Now, there was something you wanted to tell me.

TIM: Break up?! Why?! Four days ago you were telling me how great things were going.

CINDY: Tim, that was four days ago. I'm a completely different woman now. And come on, we fight all the time.

TIM: What are you talking about?

CINDY: What am I talking about? How about the other night when you said the universe is infinite and I said it ends somewhere after Pluto?

TIM: That was a fight?

CINDY: Yah! I cried when you hung up! I mean, what would we tell our kids when they ask? Mommy says one thing and Daddy says the complete opposite. They wouldn't know what to believe! They'd be stopping at green lights and bathing in dirt.

TIM: So we can't have a disagreement?

CINDY: No! I need you to be exactly the same as me.

TIM: I don't even know what to say to that.

CINDY: That's not the only thing. My independence too. Remember that time you got mad at me because I wanted to go dancing with my friends?

TIM: First of all, we had plans that night, plans you made and asked me to take the day off of work for. Second, you sprained your ankle and the doctor told you if you danced on it you may never walk again!

CINDY: Tim, we should still be in the honeymoon phase, but I haven't been happy in forever.

TIM: What? Just the other day you said, and I quote, "I'm happy and I feel like we're on a honeymoon, perhaps it's some sort of phase." This doesn't make any sense!

CINDY: Doesn't it Tim? Or does it make so much sense that it rocks your world to the ground?

TIM: What? What does that mean?

CINDY: You know how bored I get with stuff. Remember that time I tried to take up tennis? I gave that right up.

TIM: You gave it up because you sprained your ankle.

CINDY: Tim, I think you're an amazing person. I just don't think that we're amazing together. In fact, I think I actually drain some of the amazingness out of you making myself more amazing.

TIM: So that's it? It's over?

CINDY: No, no, no. We can still be really, really, really, really, really, really, really, really good friends.

TIM: Forget it. I've got plenty of friends. The last thing I need is one more.

CINDY: OK. *(She gets up.)* I should go. *(She pulls out a T-shirt from her bag:)* Here, I thought you'd want this back. Go Syracuse right?

(She tosses Tim the shirt. He looks at it, confused.)

TIM: *(Confused:)* This isn't mine.

(He hands it back to Cindy.)

CINDY: *(Pause.)* Oh. Sorry. Can I have a hug good-bye.

TIM: Why? You want one last spin on the Tim-go-round? Forget it sister.

CINDY: Good-bye Tim.

TIM: Good-bye Cindy. Going out with you is like jogging with a lemur. Just when you think you're getting somewhere, bam! You're off a cliff. *(Cindy leaves. Tim takes off his shirt and looks at his tattoo in the mirror again.)*

TIM: Crap.

END OF SCENE

Those Who Can, Do
Brighde Mullins

Dramatic

Ann Marie, an advertising executive, early thirties; Hal, an advertising executive, in his late twenties

Setting: Outside of Saatchi and Saatchi Advertising in N.Y.C. Situation: Ann Marie has returned to her former occupation after being disillusioned as a poetry professor.

HAL: I heard about your "research-slash-teaching stint" in a ghetto high school. Really gutsy and super-smart. Your street credibility is through the roof: You can say, *"I have seen gangsta style with my own eyes."* And that can go directly into client consultations. There's still plenty to be made in the White Kids With Dreadlocks Teen Sector. *Where the ghetto goes the suburbs follow.*

ANN MARIE: Where did you hear that? Is that what people are saying?

HAL: I know, I know, no matter what people are saying, you had *noble motives.* I don't doubt that. I am just putting a spin on it. I wanted to ask you something — have you been following the story about the high school English teacher who was shot by his own student? What do you think?

ANN MARIE: About what?

HAL: About kids shooting their teachers —

ANN MARIE: I'm surprised it doesn't happen more often.

HAL: There's an episode based on it on *Law and Order* tonight. Are you watching?

ANN MARIE: I hate *Law and Order.*

HAL: How can you hate *Law and Order?*
   (She imitates the "Law and Order" sound.)
   "Cha-Ching"

ANN MARIE: *Law and Order* always gets the facts wrong. They isolate some facts and de-contextualize them.

HAL: They have to do that in order to nail it to a through-line. Life has no through-line. TV has a through-line.

ANN MARIE: Anyway, how can they have a show based on that case when it hasn't gone to trial yet? What if the jurors see it?

HAL: It's very fall of the Roman Empire. The kid is tried in the court of public opinion, which is made up of these Hollywood television writers. I'll tell you what the verdict is tomorrow because I have to watch it. It's research — *Deep Image Product Placement.* You enmesh the product into the TV show itself. *(Teasing her.)* Of course, it's not as flash as being a ghetto schoolteacher.

ANN MARIE: I hate to burst your bubble, Hal, but I wasn't a ghetto schoolteacher. And it's called the inner-city, not the ghetto. *I taught English at Staten Island Community College.*

HAL: I don't think I've ever even set foot on Staten Island.

ANN MARIE: That's the kind of response that I usually get.

HAL: What's it like?

ANN MARIE: Landfills and delis. It's like nothing. It's unlike. The best thing about it is taking the ferry, twice a day, there and back. Manhattan's a diorama, blood-red sunrises, hangnail moons, the Hudson River. To get to Staten Island is free, but to get back costs you fifty cents.

HAL: That seems fair. So what was it like being a professor?

ANN MARIE: I was stalked by a student, harassed by colleagues, underpaid, overworked, and for what?

HAL: You tell me. If you weren't doing it as research, why were you doing it?

ANN MARIE: I wanted to do something meaningful — also, and this is something I've only discussed with my shrink, but: I thought that I could start writing poetry again.

HAL: But why couldn't you just write poetry and work here?

ANN MARIE: They seem antithetical to me.

HAL: Poetry and Advertising?

ANN MARIE: Opposite ends of the continuum of human expression.

HAL: Not at all.

ANN MARIE: Oh, come on!

HAL: Think about it: In two thousand years do you think people will be reading what today's poets are writing?

ANN MARIE: Rap is the new poetry, Springsteen is the new Shakespeare?

HAL: No. I think that if there is any civilization left in two thousand years, then Poetry Scholars will be studying "plop, plop, fizz, fizz." They'll be writing papers about the vale of soul making in "ring around the collar," and teaching courses around "you're soaking in it." That's the new poetry. The real poetry is happening right here, Ann Marie, and you were always writing it.

ANN MARIE: If you do believe that, and I'm not sure that you do —

HAL: *(Overriding her.)* Hey, I have an M.F.A. from Brown. Of course I believe it.

ANN MARIE: Is that true, do you *really* believe it?

HAL: Yes, it's "true," yes, I really believe it!

ANN MARIE: Did you just put air-quotation-marks around the word *true?*

HAL: Yes, I did.

ANN MARIE: Thereby negating the word TRUE, or underlying the ironic meaning of the concept of TRUTH itself as a construct?

HAL: Hey, whoa professor, we aren't in the Ivory Tower now.

ANN MARIE: Funnily enough the Chair of the Creative Writing Department was always talking about the similarities between teaching and advertising.

HAL: And?

ANN MARIE: It's just funny.

HAL: So wait, I just want to go back to this image that I have of you as a professor: I'm seeing you in a tweed skirt, tight bun, a nubby blazer. And I bet your students got little crushes on you and followed you around? Am I right?

ANN MARIE: Funnily enough, you are. Do you ever feel like your life is composed of unfinished business?

END OF SCENE

Tourist Attraction
Craig Pospisil

Comic
Jason and Nancy, twenties

> *A subway car. Jason, an actor, sits and reads a play script. The train pulls into the station and the doors open. Nancy, a giddy tourist, gets on. She smiles broadly and gleefully as she takes in the car. She sees Jason.*

NANCY: Oh, this is so exciting!

JASON: *(Looking around the car:)* Uh, . . . what?

NANCY: A real New York City subway!

JASON: Oh. Yeah.

NANCY: Do you ride the train every day?

JASON: Yeah, sure.

NANCY: Wow! Wow. How do you stand it?

JASON: What?

NANCY: The excitement, the exhilaration of it all.

JASON: *(Slight pause.)* It's just the subway.

NANCY: Just the — ! Oh!

JASON: What?

NANCY: You're one of them!

JASON: One of who?

NANCY: A real New Yorker. A jaded New Yorker. Wow!

JASON: If you say so.

NANCY: Oh, that's perfect. Perfect. That New York wit. *(Slight pause.)* Can I have your autograph?

JASON: Huh? I'm just a guy on the train. Why would you want my autograph?

NANCY: To show my friends when I get home to Boca Raton. That means "Mouth of the Rat."

JASON: Oh. Great.

NANCY: So, what do you do?

JASON: I'm an actor.

NANCY: There! See! I thought you looked familiar. Oh, please give me your autograph.

JASON: No.

NANCY: Why not?

JASON: Because I'm no one, OK? You don't want my fucking autograph!
    (Silence.)

NANCY: I'm sorry.

JASON: *(Pause.)* No, look, I . . . I'm sorry I shouted.

NANCY: It's OK.

JASON: No, it's not. I'm sorry. OK?

NANCY: Sure.

JASON: Great.

NANCY: *(Pause.)* Excuse me?

JASON: Yeah?

NANCY: Would you take my picture? A picture of me here on the A train?

JASON: Sure.
    (Nancy pulls out a camera. Jason takes it and points it at her.)

NANCY: Oh, wait, wait. *(She quickly fixes her hair or makes herself up, etc.)*
    Where should I stand?

JASON: Uh, . . . how 'bout in front of the map.

NANCY: Oh, yeah. Great.
    (Nancy goes to the map and poses. Jason raises the camera.)

NANCY: Wait.

JASON: What?

NANCY: Where are we? On the map.

JASON: We're, uh, right about here.

NANCY: All right. I'm gonna point there!

JASON: Sure. Good idea. You ready?

NANCY: Yeah!
    (She poses again, playfully pointing at where they are on the map. Jason takes the picture, and then starts to hand it back to her.)

NANCY: Oh, one more. One more please.

JASON: *(Sighs.)* All right. One more.

NANCY: Where should I stand?

JASON: I don't know.

NANCY: What's really New York-y?

JASON: The map.

NANCY: But other than that.

JASON: Ah, I . . . OK, I know. Lie down on the seats and pretend you're asleep.

NANCY: Pretend I'm sleeping?

JASON: Nothing says New York like someone sleeping on the subway.

NANCY: OK, yeah.

(Nancy lies down on the seats. Jason moves about looking for the best place to take the picture from.)

JASON: Hey, open your mouth a little.

NANCY: What?

JASON: Like you've passed out from drinking too much Thunderbird.

NANCY: Oh! Got it.

(Nancy gets into the part, sprawling more, mouth open. Jason snaps a picture.)

JASON: OK, here you go.

NANCY: Thank you so much!

JASON: Sure.

(Jason goes back to his script. Nancy snaps some pictures of the car. Then she takes Jason's picture.)

JASON: Did you just take my picture?

NANCY: No.

JASON: Yes, you did.

NANCY: No, no. I was taking a picture of that sign.

JASON: The one behind my head?

NANCY: *(Slight pause.)* Maybe.

JASON: Why'd you take my picture?

NANCY: I just want to be able to show my friends the famous New York actor I met on the subway.

JASON: I'm not famous. Nothing like it.

NANCY: I know I've seen you.

JASON: No, you haven't.

NANCY: I'm sure I have.

JASON: No, you haven't. Now do you mind? I'm trying to read!

NANCY: *(Pause.)* Weren't you on *Law and Order*?

JASON: No.

NANCY: Then it was that Burger King commercial.

JASON: No, no, no. You haven't seen me. I haven't been on any of those.

NANCY: Then where —

JASON: Nowhere, OK?! You haven't seen me anywhere. I've been pounding the pavement ever since I got to this town, but I haven't been cast in anything on TV, or in the movies, or on Broadway, or Off-Broadway! The last thing I did was a ten-minute play in a grungy thirty-five seat theater in a basement off Avenue A. And that's nowhere you'll ever see. So leave me alone!!

(Silence. Then Jason and Nancy shift as the train comes to a stop in the tunnel.)

JASON: Aw, damn it! Not now.

NANCY: Is it supposed to stop in the middle of the tunnel?

JASON: No, it just knows I'm trying to get to an audition.

NANCY: You're going to an audition? Right now? What's it for?

JASON: A play.

NANCY: What's it called?

JASON: *Months on End*

NANCY: Is it good?

JASON: Who knows.

NANCY: Haven't you read it?

JASON: *(Holding up the script he's been trying to read:)* How can I?

NANCY: Oh. Sorry. *(Pause.)* Well, hey, maybe I could help you.

JASON: How?

NANCY: I could help you memorize your lines.

JASON: I'm just reading from the script. I don't have to memorize it.

NANCY: Then I could read it with you.

JASON: On the train?

NANCY: Sure.

JASON: No, thanks.

NANCY: I used to act in high school.

JASON: Really.

NANCY: Yeah. People said I was really good. I was in *Fiddler on the Roof.*

JASON: That's terrific. But I need to go over this scene, OK?

NANCY: All right, look, I'm sorry, OK? But, . . . but I get a little claustrophobic sometimes and . . . and this is making me nervous. I mean,
   I know nothing's really wrong, right? But, I mean, . . . how long's
   the train gonna be stopped?

JASON: No one ever knows. *(Slight pause.)* Don't worry. It'll start again.

NANCY: Uh-huh, OK, yeah. I'm sure it's fine. Probably. I mean —

JASON: Hey, look, you wanna read with me?

NANCY: Really?

JASON: Yeah.

NANCY: That'd be great!

JASON: *(Showing her the script:)* OK, here, you read —

NANCY: *(Reading.)* "Jenna, hi! I'm Tony. Sorry I'm —"

JASON: No. "Tony" is my part. You read Phoebe.

NANCY: Oh.

   *(They read from the script and begin to connect and flirt a bit just as
   the characters in the scene do.)*

JASON AS TONY: Jenna, hi! I'm Tony. Sorry I'm late. All the snow slowed
   me down. Listen, I hope you don't have plans tonight, 'cause I had
   this wild impulse on the way over here and I stopped at Lincoln Center and got two tickets for the ballet. I thought we could go for a
   drink first, then to the ballet, and then I made reservations for a late
   dinner at the Supper Club. They're gonna have a swing band, and I
   thought we could have some great food and a few passes on the dance
   floor. *(Slight pause.)* Whadya say?

NANCY AS PHOEBE: Well, . . . ah, that sounds great, . . . but . . .

JASON AS TONY: What?

NANCY AS PHOEBE: I'm not Jenna.

JASON AS TONY: *(Slight pause.)* But you're wearing a red scarf.

NANCY AS PHOEBE: Well, it's cold out. And I'm still not Jenna.

JASON AS TONY: *(Slight pause.)* Right, OK, well, thanks. Sorry I bothered
   you. God, what an idiot.

NANCY AS PHOEBE: Oh, no, I thought it was lovely.

JASON AS TONY: Really?

NANCY AS PHOEBE: Yeah.

JASON AS TONY: Oh, you don't know how long I spent trying to think of something that would really grab you. I mean, her. *(Slight pause.)* You think it'll work?

NANCY AS PHOEBE: Yeah, sure. I'd go out with you.

(They break out of the scene slowly.)

JASON: OK. OK, well, that's all I have to read for the audition so . . . That was good.

NANCY: Wow, that was so much fun! Hey, what do you think, . . . should I move here and become an actress?

JASON: Ah, . . . I don't know.

NANCY: *(Smiles.)* No. Yeah, I was kidding. *(Slight pause.)* I really liked your reading.

JASON: Thanks. I think I'd be good in the part. But you never know what people are looking for.

(Jason stands close to Nancy, staring deeply into her eyes.)

Of course, we might be stuck here for a while.

(The train lurches forward, throwing Jason and Nancy into each others' arms for support. They hold for a moment, and then Nancy becomes uncomfortable.)

NANCY: Hey, look at that. Train's moving.

JASON: I know.

NANCY: Uh-huh, yeah, see, ah, I'm claustrophobic.

(Jason releases her, and they separate.)

NANCY: Well, . . . I'll look for you on TV. I bet you'll be famous and I'll be able to tell people, "I got stuck on the subway with him." Not that they'll believe me.

JASON: Gimme your camera.

NANCY: What?

JASON: Just gimme your camera.

(Nancy takes it out and hands it to Jason. He puts his arm around her and holds the camera out, extended, with his other arm. They put on big smiles and Jason takes a picture of them together.)

NANCY: Thanks.

(Jason gives her back the camera and reaches into his bag. He pulls out a headshot and quickly signs it.)

JASON: What's your name?

NANCY: Nancy.

JASON: Well, here, Nancy. For what it's worth.

NANCY: Oh, wow. Thanks, I . . . wait . . . Jason Clark? I know that name. Did you ever work in Florida?

JASON: Hmm? Ah, . . . no. Oh, and here's my stop.

NANCY: Wait a minute . . . ! You were a Mouseketeer!!

JASON: No, I wasn't!

NANCY: Yes, you were! You're little Jason Clark! I can't believe it! When I was twelve I was totally in love with you! Ohmigod!!

(The train pulls into the 42nd Street stop. Jason hurries to the doors.)

JASON: Come on, come on!

NANCY: Will you kiss me?

JASON: Open up!!

(The doors open and Jason runs for his life with Nancy chasing after him.)

NANCY: I love you, Jason!!!

END OF SCENE

Tumor
Sheila Callaghan

Comic
Kathie, twenty-nine; Pete, mid-thirties

> *Kathie and Pete are browsing in a supermarket. They are both very*
> *pregnant. They catch sight of one another and begin eyeing one an-*
> *other's bellies stealthily and not altogether pleasantly. They do sev-*
> *eral "inconspicuous" turns around one another before Pete speaks.*

PETE: How long?

KATHIE: Two more months. And you?

PETE: The same. Boy or girl?

KATHIE: Don't know yet. We decided not to find out. You?

PETE: Girl.

KATHIE: How nice. Picked out a name yet?

PETE: Several. I'm vacillating between Skylar Raven, Prairie Raven, and Prairie Sunrise

KATHIE: How lovely.

PETE: I didn't want her to grow up thinking she was average

KATHIE: Of course not

PETE: Are you going natural

KATHIE: No, we opted for the epidural. I'm not good with pain

PETE: Well, I figured since little Skylar Prairie has been all squished up inside me for nine months with no choice in the matter, I could endure a little discomfort for her sake

KATHIE: Very courageous of you

PETE: Not courageous. Human.

KATHIE: And how is your partner handling everything

PETE: I'm a single mom

KATHIE: Oh, I'm sorry

PETE: Not at all

KATHIE: I could never ever do this alone, Richard has been so supportive

throughout everything, he waits on me hand and foot, goes to the
store for me at crazy hours, puts up with my violent mood swings

PETE: He sounds like a treasure

KATHIE: I'd lose my mind without him. Right now he's out shopping for
a crib.

PETE: I couldn't help noticing, I hope I'm not being too forward

KATHIE: Please

PETE: You put dog shampoo in your basket

KATHIE: We have a dog

PETE: It's toxic. I've been doing some reading. Continued exposure of your
skin to those chemicals might put your baby at risk of being born
without a spine

KATHIE: No

PETE: They've done studies

KATHIE: That's horrific

PETE: And that bottled water

KATHIE: Yes?

PETE: It's not from the alps. It's from Vermont. A small town called Brat-
tleboro. The inhabitants let their livestock drink from the mountain
streams and contaminate the water supply. In the early eighties a rash
of babies from the surrounding area was born wearing bifocals.

KATHIE: What about these grapes

PETE: Certain pesticides have been known to cause infantile derision dis-
order

KATHIE: Which is

PETE: A child without a sense of irony

KATHIE: Dear lord, I had no idea

PETE: Not many people do. It's a noxious world. We've got to be careful.

KATHIE: No doubt . . . thanks for the info

PETE: Any time . . .

(Pete exits. Kathie stares at her bottled water.)

END OF SCENE

Twenty Years Ago
Frederick Stroppel

Comic
Eddie and Joan, thirty-eight

> *Eddie and Joan are at a high school reunion. Eddie thinks Joan is somebody else.*

EDDIE: Melanie!

(Joan turns and looks at Eddie.)

JOAN: Pardon me?

EDDIE: Melanie Hawthorne! I can't believe it! *(Joan looks at him with bewilderment.)* You don't recognize me, do you? Ed Gottlieb. Eddie. *(He proudly displays his name-tag on his jacket lapel.)*

JOAN: I'm afraid there's some mistake . . .

EDDIE: No, it's me. It really is. I lost sixty pounds. *(He opens his jacket to show off his slimmed-down waist. There are several pens in his shirt pocket, and an ink stain underneath.)* See? Nobody recognizes me. It's amazing.

JOAN: No, I mean, you've mistaken me for someone else.

EDDIE: Oh, I could never mistake that smile. Or those green eyes. Gee, you haven't changed a bit. How are you?

JOAN: I'm fine, but . . .

EDDIE: You know the last time I saw you? Jill Simon's party. Remember that? Twenty years ago!

JOAN: What I'm saying is, I'm not who you think I am. My name isn't Melanie.

EDDIE: *(Laughs.)* Yeah, right.

JOAN: It isn't. My name is Joan. You don't know me. I never went to this school.

EDDIE: That's funny. You always had a quick wit. I remember that about you.

JOAN: No, seriously, this isn't my reunion.

EDDIE: I felt that way myself at first. You know, I wasn't the most popular guy at school, I admit that. I was a loner. Not that I wanted to be, it just sort of worked out that way. So I figured, maybe I shouldn't go to the reunion. But then I figured, who knows where I'll be in twenty years? I could be dead, right? *(He giggles.)* So I came. And I'm glad I did. I'm glad you came, Melanie.

JOAN: I'm not Melanie. My name is Joan Peterford. I married Henry Peterford. Hank Peterford.

EDDIE: *(With some surprise.)* You married Hank Peterford?

JOAN: He's doing the Hokey-Pokey in there, even as we speak.

EDDIE: I thought Hank married someone from upstate.

JOAN: He did! He married me! I'm from Syracuse. That's where we live. It's a six-hour drive.

EDDIE: See, I got that mixed up. So you got married down here, and then you moved up to Syracuse.

JOAN: No! I got married in Syracuse, and I never moved anywhere. I've never even been in this town before.

EDDIE: I know, it's really changed, hasn't it? Did you see the new movie theater?

JOAN: Yes, I did, but . . .

EDDIE: That little camera store next to the theater? You want to know who owns that? Me! Yes! Always wanted to own a camera store. One of my childhood dreams.

JOAN: Congratulations.

EDDIE: You gotta take care of your dreams. I promised myself, by the time of my twenty-year reunion, I'd have my own business, and I'd have a size 34 waist. *(Patting his waist.)* Gettin' there. How about yourself? I notice you've rounded out a little. More buxom.

JOAN: Actually I haven't gained a pound in ten years.

EDDIE: No, don't let it bother you. It's very becoming. I always said you were a little too thin. Not that I actually said that. It wasn't my place to say that. If I'd been going out with you, maybe I would have . . . said . . . *(Anxious.)* You don't remember me, do you?

JOAN: I can't remember you! I've never met you!

EDDIE: Right. We didn't travel in the same circles. I mean, you were a cheerleader, and on the Student Council, and you wrote for the school paper — you were too busy to notice me. I was always hanging out in the Audio-Visual room anyway. I don't blame you for forgetting me. I wasn't that memorable.

JOAN: Look, Johnnie . . .

EDDIE: Eddie.

JOAN: Eddie . . . I don't know how to get this across to you, but you're confusing me with someone else. I was not in your class, I was never a cheerleader, and we've never seen each other before. It's as simple as that. Maybe your friend is inside. *(Joan checks the name-tags.)* What was her name? Hawthorne? *(Finding the name-tag.)* Melanie Hawthorne. See, she's not even here. She probably stayed home. I wish I'd stayed home.

EDDIE: *(Taking the sticker.)* Would you like me to put this on for you?

JOAN: No!

EDDIE: I'll be careful . . .

JOAN: What is your problem? Listen carefully . . . *(Pointing to the name-tag.)* This is not me. This has nothing to do with me.

EDDIE: *(Understanding.)* You shouldn't be ashamed of a little extra weight. That comes naturally with age. Hey, otherwise, you look great. You could pass for thirty-five easily.

JOAN: I'm thirty-three!

EDDIE: That's the spirit. I know I let my weight become a problem for me when I was in school. It was a social crutch, you know? My therapist tells me . . .

JOAN: Eddie, it was a pleasure meeting you, but my husband is waiting for me, I think we have to do the Bunny Hop or something . . .

EDDIE: You always were a good dancer. I remember you at the Senior Ball, when you were doing the can-can on one of the tables.

JOAN: Was I . . . ?

EDDIE: You were a little tipsy, I think. Kicking your legs way up in the air, those long slender legs . . . I didn't actually have a date for the Senior Ball myself, but I was one of the photographers.

JOAN: *(Trying to edge away from him.)* Is that so?

EDDIE: I still do some photography on the side. Had some pictures published in the local paper. And last year I was in *Newsday*, when the lumber yard burned down. The heat was so intense it warped my lens cap.

JOAN: How interesting . . .

(Joan is about to escape, but Eddie enthusiastically circles around her.)

EDDIE: You don't know how many pictures I took of you in school. Mostly when you weren't looking. But nothing embarrassing. They were all wonderful shots. You were my favorite subject, Melanie. If you only knew . . .

JOAN: Once and for all, my name isn't Melanie. It's just not. Start with this fact, and build from it.

EDDIE: *(Smiling indulgently.)* I like it when you tease me.

(Joan takes out her wallet.)

JOAN: *(Showing her license.)* Look. Joan. Joan Peterford. From Syracuse. See?

EDDIE: Not a great picture.

JOAN: *(Producing credit cards.)* My MasterCard. My Visa. Joan. Joan. Joan.

EDDIE: *(Beat.)* So you changed your name to Joan?

JOAN: My name has always been Joan.

EDDIE: "Melanie" is so much prettier.

JOAN: Look. See my birth date? I'm thirty-three.

EDDIE: *(Pondering this.)* 1972? That doesn't make sense. *(Concerned.)* Are you like in a witness-protection program?

JOAN: *(Her exasperation peaking.)* I'm a different human being! I'm a creature you've never met before! If I look like this Melanie Hawthorne, it's a complete and total coincidence. We have no connection, we are not linked genetically or spiritually, she is Melanie, I am Joan, we are separate entities with separate lives. We do not coexist in the same space. This is my body, and there's no one here with me. Period. the end.

EDDIE: You're not into that Scientology stuff, are you? They can totally fuck with your mind. Excuse my language.

JOAN: *(Defeated.)* I have to go.

EDDIE: *(Accommodating.)* I'll wait.

JOAN: I won't be back.

EDDIE: I thought maybe we could have a dance later . . .

JOAN: I don't think so.

EDDIE: For old times' sake . . .

JOAN: *(Quite definitely.)* No. No.

EDDIE: *(Wounded, sadly.)* Oh. I get it. OK.

(Eddie turns away. Joan observes the hangdog expression on his face with some sympathy.)

JOAN: It's nothing personal. *(Pause.)* I don't dance, anyway. The can-can, or anything else.

EDDIE: Things don't change all that much in twenty years, do they?

JOAN: I'm not who you think I am. Really. *(Eddie doesn't respond.)* Well . . . My husband . . . *(Joan starts to leave.)*

EDDIE: Hank Peterford, huh? So he wound up with you after all. I guess I shouldn't be surprised. *(Indicating the name-tag.)* Mind if I hold on to this?

JOAN: *(Turning back to him, intrigued.)* What do you mean?

EDDIE: As a souvenir . . .

JOAN: No, I mean . . . about Hank. Not being a surprise.

EDDIE: Well, you and Hank . . .

JOAN: Yes?

EDDIE: Anyway, it was great seeing you again, Melanie . . .

JOAN: *(Now very interested.)* Wait a minute . . . Me and Hank? What are you saying? Are you saying that we were involved?

EDDIE: If that's what you want to call it.

JOAN: What would you call it?

EDDIE: That was twenty years ago. I don't dwell on the past. Tomorrow is another day. My therapist says . . .

JOAN: Let's dwell on the past for a just a minute. You're saying I used to go out with Hank Peterford? Melanie Hawthorne? I was, like, his girl?

EDDIE: Well, yeah. Weren't you?

JOAN: But — was it serious? Was it your basic high school romance, or was it . . . more?

EDDIE: I would say it was more. A lot more. *(Joan looks into the main hall.)* Of course you would have a more informed perspective on the subject, being an active participant, as it were.

(Joan waves to her husband inside with a steely smile.)

JOAN: *(To herself.)* That's right, wave, you sneaky son-of-a-bitch. Had to come to the reunion, didn't you? Had to drive six hours . . . *(To Eddie.)* You married, Eddie?

EDDIE: No, I've never had the privilege.

JOAN: It's an educational experience. You think you know someone, and then you think maybe you don't know him as well as you thought, and then you find out you knew him better than you could have imagined. *(Muttering.)* Waiting for the Viennese table . . . !

EDDIE: Are you feeling all right, Melanie?

JOAN: I'm not Melanie!

EDDIE: You seem to have a real problem in dealing with your past.

JOAN: You're right. I'm having a memory block. Can't remember a thing. Help me out. What exactly happened twenty years ago?

EDDIE: You really don't remember?

JOAN: Selective amnesia. A total blank.

EDDIE: Maybe you need to see a doctor.

JOAN: I need you, Eddie. You. *(Eddie is immensely flattered.)* Tell me everything about it. About them. About us.

EDDIE: *(Catching on.)* I get it. This is a test, right? You want to see how much I really know about you. OK, I'll show you . . . *(Concentrating.)* Let's see, I remember the first time I saw you, the beginning of Senior year, you were in my homeroom. God, what a pretty girl you were. You'd just transferred from Syosset, your parents bought the house on Gruber Drive where the Caseys used to live . . . In Syosset you had an A-minus average, you belonged to the French Club and the National Honor Society, and you played Emily in *Our Town* — pretty good for a junior, the lead and everything . . . Does any of this sound familiar?

JOAN: Vaguely.

EDDIE: I know about Syosset because I used to help Mr. Liggero in the main office on Friday afternoons, and whenever he stepped out I could check all the transcripts . . . I knew everybody's grades. I know what you did in middle school, and kindergarten, and when you had the measles, and how you scored on the Stanford-Binet tests. You know what your I.Q. is? 135. Mine is pretty high, too. Higher than Hank's.

JOAN: Yeah, getting back to Hank . . . So I was the new girl, and I went out with him . . .

EDDIE: You were the new girl, and you were just so pretty, so intelligent, vivacious, talented . . . All the guys were crazy about you. All the girls hated you.

JOAN: *(Drily.)* I can't imagine why.

EDDIE: They thought you were a show-off, and they were jealous. But once they got to know you, and realized what a super person you were inside . . . You were voted Most Popular and Best Personality, you know.

JOAN: I must have been quite a babe.

EDDIE: You were the most magical, wonderful . . . *(Embarrassed.)* Maybe I'm talking out of turn, but I promised myself I would say this to you tonight if I saw you. I've waited for the opportunity for the longest time, Melanie, and even though it's too late now, I still want you to know how much I . . . I've always . . . *(Hedging.)* . . . admired you . . .

JOAN: *(Not interested, pressing on.)* So Hank was crazy about me too, I imagine.

EDDIE: Hank . . . ? Well, at that time he was still going out with Debbie Persky . . .

JOAN: Debbie Persky?

EDDIE: You remember her, with the long blonde hair down to her . . . *(Eddie gestures.)* Always wore a headband. They had an on-and-off relationship. Hank was always looking for something better.

JOAN: He was that type, huh?

EDDIE: So he and Debbie were always battling. They had one fight in the lunchroom — it might have been over you — Food flying . . . Milk containers . . .

JOAN: *(Glancing into the main hall.)* Debbie Persky . . . *(To Eddie.)* Do you have a pen? *(Eddie hands her a pen from his shirt pocket. Joan writes the name on a cocktail napkin.)* Who else did he go out with? Just out of curiosity.

EDDIE: Let me think . . . there was Lori Butz: B-U-T-Z . . . and Mindy Schwartzanappel . . . *(He begs off spelling it.)* And Kathy Callan . . . twice . . . *(Joan underlines the name twice.)* And Sherry

Malinowski . . . I don't know if I should be telling you all this. I mean, Hank and I . . .

JOAN: He'll never know where it came from. Your friendship is safe. *(Realizing, irritated.)* He introduced me to someone named Sherry tonight, too.

EDDIE: That's just it. There was no friendship. We weren't sworn enemies, but . . . He was always passing some remark about my weight, or the way I walked . . . And he wouldn't let me join the *Honeymooners* Fan Club. I remember that — he blackballed me. I knew more about the *Honeymooners* than anybody. *(Mastering his resentment.)* However . . .

JOAN: All in the past.

EDDIE: Right.

JOAN: *(Leading him along.)* So after Debbie Persky, Hank started going out with me . . .

EDDIE: Just after you made the cheerleading squad. I was in charge of videotaping the games. I still have some tapes of you in your red-and-gold outfit . . . *(Defensively.)* In the attic somewhere. I don't watch them anymore. Yeah, Hank was on the football team. He was no star, by any means, but he looked good in his uniform. I guess you found him glamorous.

JOAN: So if that was in the fall, that means we were going out the whole school year.

EDDIE: And the next summer. Everyone figured you were going to get married. They thought you were the perfect couple.

JOAN: What did you think?

EDDIE: I shouldn't . . . *(Changing his mind.)* No, I promised myself I wouldn't hide anything. I promised I'd tell you how I felt. *(Speaking out.)* I thought it was all wrong. He wasn't nearly good enough for you. He didn't appreciate you. He thought you were just another girl.

JOAN: Maybe I was, Eddie. You shouldn't have these dreamy notions about women. We're only human.

EDDIE: No. You were special. But he didn't recognize it. I remember one time after gym, when he was telling his friends how he . . . you know . . . had 'fun' with you. *(Lowering his voice.)* Sex, you know?

JOAN: He was bragging about it?

EDDIE: He was saying . . . Well, I won't get specific, because he's your husband now, but . . . let me just say, I found it disgusting. I wanted to
go over there and knock him down and tell him he was a stupid, in-
sensitive . . . asshole. I'm sorry, that's what he was. Maybe he's
changed.

JOAN: But you didn't say anything.

EDDIE: It wasn't really my business. But I would have never treated you
that way. I would never have such disrespect. I would have been happy
just to worship you.

JOAN: So Hank and I went out for a year or so, and had all kinds of "fun,"
and then we broke up. Was it another girl? *(With pen poised.)* What
was her name?

EDDIE: I can't believe you don't remember any of this.

JOAN: It's coming back slowly. You're being an enormous help.

EDDIE: What about the Senior Ball? You must remember that.

JOAN: Sure. I was doing the can-can.

EDDIE: But when you and Hank were voted King and Queen . . . and
you danced to "Over the Rainbow" . . . They had one of those ball-
room chandeliers throwing off the different colored lights . . . I have
it all on film.

JOAN: I'd like to see it someday.

EDDIE: *(Pointing to his head.)* I have it up here, too. I don't know how
many times I've replayed it over the years. How many times I've
wished . . . You were so beautiful that night. Drifting across the floor
in an ice-blue gown, with your cheek resting against a white orchid,
and sprigs of baby's-breath nestled in your hair . . . Like an angel.
Like a dream.

JOAN: Blue is a good color for me.

EDDIE: It was a pure moment. So often now, when I'm depressed or defeated, I think about that moment of purity, and it restores me. It
gives me hope . . . It must be flattering, to know that you can affect
someone so powerfully, twenty years later.

JOAN: It's very gratifying. *(Impatiently pushing on.)* So now it's summer,
we've all graduated, we're looking forward to college . . .

EDDIE: That was a great summer. Man, the parties . . . ! I didn't go to too many, but I heard about them. Claude Briscoe's pool party, when everyone was skinny-dipping, and they called the police . . . ?

JOAN: A blast. But Hank and I were starting to have problems, I'll bet.

EDDIE: I used to see you at the beach. You had a white bathing suit that summer. One piece. You never wore a bikini. You could have, but you were too classy. You wouldn't skinny-dip.

JOAN: You're wandering, Eddie. Keep the focus.

EDDIE: You used to swim along the ropes, back and forth, your long graceful arms slicing through the waves . . .

JOAN: *(Stopping him.)* Eddie! The breakup — what happened?

EDDIE: *(Hesitant.)* I don't think I should talk about that.

JOAN: Why not?

EDDIE: It's too personal.

JOAN: You promised yourself you wouldn't hide anything, remember?

EDDIE: It was all rumor — maybe none of it was true. I mean, I never saw the ring.

JOAN: The ring?

EDDIE: You were going off to college, anyway. Wellesley. So you'd be living apart. What was the point?

JOAN: You mean, like an engagement ring?

EDDIE: Hank had no money. It wasn't practical.

JOAN: Tell me we didn't get married.

EDDIE: No, of course not. And that other thing — I never believed that anyway. I saw you at the beach every day, and I never noticed any change.

JOAN: The other thing?

EDDIE: *(Embarrassed.)* You know. *(Gestures to his stomach.)*

JOAN: *(Slowly understanding.)* Oh . . . Let me get this straight. He proposed to me, and then he knocked me up, and then he left me? *(Looking into the hall.)* A prince. A fucking prince.

EDDIE: Come on, Melanie, be fair. It was you.

JOAN: Me?

EDDIE: Not that I blame you. Why would you want to tie yourself down? You had your whole future waiting. And he didn't deserve you. What could he give you?

JOAN: *(Pleased.)* You mean I broke off with him? Really?

EDDIE: He was so sure of himself. He thought it would last forever.

JOAN: I really burned him?

EDDIE: At Jill Simon's party. Just before you left for college.

JOAN: Tell me. Tell me.

EDDIE: It must have been about one o'clock in the morning. Everybody inside was pretty stoned. You guys went for one of those long walks, and I was there outside when you came back — I was sort of by the side of the house, near some bushes — and I couldn't hear exactly what you were saying but I could tell that Hank was really upset. You were talking in the driveway for a while, really quiet, and then he started talking louder, and he started yelling and cursing, and calling you names, and he started to shake you — I was ready to jump him if he hit you, I swear — and all the time you stood there, regally, like a goddess, calmly taking his abuse — magnificent — if only I could have taken a picture . . . And when he finally stopped, when he finally gave up, you just turned and walked away. Walked away into the night. The next day you left for Wellesley, and I never saw you again. Until today. Until now.

JOAN: And what did Hank do?

EDDIE: He just stayed there in the driveway for a long time, just stood there, crying.

JOAN: *(Surprised.)* Crying? Hank?

EDDIE: Like his heart was breaking. Like everything was breaking inside of him. I kind of felt sorry for him. He was all alone. It's tough to be alone.

(Beat.)

JOAN: And the baby?

EDDIE: I think you lost it. Or something. *(Shrugging.)* Like I said, ancient history. You have to put it out of your mind. That was Hank's problem, see? He couldn't get over you. Every time I saw him after that night, he was with someone who looked like you. You know: brunette, pretty, stylish . . . The only type of girl he wanted to date. Like he was trying to replace you. Not that he could. They were all pale imitations. There's only one Melanie. How could he ever love anyone else? I couldn't.

(Joan steps away; she needs time to get this information straight in her head. Eddie gives her a moment.)

EDDIE: So you're surprised, right? You didn't think I knew so much about you, did you? I know your birthday, and your social security number . . . I still remember your old phone number on Gruber Drive. Confession: I used to call you all the time, but then I'd hang up. *(Nodding.)* That was me. Silly, huh? Couldn't even say hello. I was so afraid of you. You were so . . . perfect. *(Joan says nothing.)* And then when your parents moved again, I thought I'd never see you again, I'd never get the chance . . . I drove up to Wellesley one weekend, you know. Yes. I went to the registrar, and I found out where you were living, and I walked right up to your door. You might have been standing right on the other side. That close. *(Reassuring her.)* I don't want it to sound creepy. I mean, I didn't keep a scrapbook, or steal your underwear or anything. I just wanted you to know me. And how I felt. But I was afraid. *(With confidence.)* I'm not like that anymore. I'm a successful person now. I have my own business. I have a nice apartment. I'm altogether different. *(Earnestly.)* I'm glad you don't remember me, Melanie. I don't want you to remember. I want you to meet me now for the first time, and see me the way I am.

END OF SCENE

Untold Crimes of Insomniacs

Janet Allard

Dramatic
Goth-Girl and Ghost-Boy, both teens

> *In the graveyard. 4:35 A.M. Two meet by chance. The world spins*
> *in strange ways.*

> *(Lights up on Goth-Girl and Ghost-Boy in the graveyard.)*

GHOST-BOY: What are you doing? Is that a knife?

GOTH-GIRL: Shit! What the fuck.

GHOST-BOY: Did I scare you?

GOTH-GIRL: I thought you were a fucking Ghost.

GHOST-BOY: What if I am?

GOTH-GIRL: Are you gonna rape me or something? Steal my donuts?

GHOST-BOY: No.

GOTH-GIRL: Why not? You scared of me?

GHOST-BOY: What? You want me to rape you?

GOTH-GIRL: See how sharp this knife is? I'd cut your heart out and eat it.

GHOST-BOY: Go ahead. I don't have a heart anyway. I'm a ghost.

GOTH-GIRL: Liar.

GHOST-BOY: What were you doing? Sacrificing yourself

GOTH-GIRL: What if I was?

GHOST-BOY: I'd stop you.

GOTH-GIRL: I'm cutting myself.

GHOST-BOY: Does that hurt?

GOTH-GIRL: Do you want to try it?

GHOST-BOY: You want a donut? Lemon-filled?

GOTH-GIRL: You want a chocolate frosted?

> *(He holds out a bag of donuts. She holds out a bag of donuts. They ex-*
> *change donuts.)*

GHOST-BOY: Is this your place?

GOTH-GIRL: It's a public place.

GHOST-BOY: If you climb the fence.

GOTH-GIRL: When did you die, Ghosty?

GHOST-BOY: Hypothetically, tonight.

GOTH-GIRL: Why are you dead?

GHOST-BOY: Long story.

GOTH-GIRL: Tell me.

GHOST-BOY: I don't even know you.

GOTH-GIRL: So it should be easy.

GHOST-BOY: I fucked my step-mom.

GOTH-GIRL: Wow. Oedipal. Tonight?

GHOST-BOY: Yeah, I'm dead meat. Can't go home, I'm just walking around numb. Stupid.

How 'bout you? You dead?

GOTH-GIRL: Not yet. What time is it?

GHOST-BOY: Why? You got somewhere to be?

GOTH-GIRL: Why would I tell you, Oedipus?

GHOST-BOY: Because I asked.

GOTH-GIRL: I've got sister trouble. My sister, she's a bitch. I can't stomach her. She's always been the baby. She doesn't feel any pain, man. She's perfect. Little Miss Perfection. I'm sick of her.

GHOST-BOY: Can I tell you something else?

GOTH-GIRL: Are you really a ghost? You look pretty solid up close.

GHOST-BOY: I can't feel anything. I'm see-through. Empty. If you touched me your hand would go right through me. I'm full of nothing.

GOTH-GIRL: Maybe you're full of shit.

GHOST-BOY: You think?

GOTH-GIRL: What if I grabbed your balls? Kicked you in the stomach?

GHOST-BOY: Nothing affects me.

GOTH-GIRL: I can affect you.

GHOST-BOY: Try. I'm cold glass, baby. Impermeable.

GOTH-GIRL: How do you know?

(She holds the knife up.)

GOTH-GIRL: Are you scared of your own blood?

GHOST-BOY: Nope. Cold-blooded.

GOTH-GIRL: Are you scared of my blood? Did you ever drink someone's blood?

GHOST-BOY: All the time. No. Never.

GOTH-GIRL: Do you want to drink mine?

GHOST-BOY: Um.

GOTH-GIRL: Um?

GHOST-BOY: Yes.

GOTH-GIRL: It's not like getting a tattoo you know.

GHOST-BOY: I know.

GOTH-GIRL: This is irreversible —

GHOST-BOY: I know.

GOTH-GIRL: You can't wake up from this.

GHOST-BOY: I don't want to.

GOTH-GIRL: Say what I say.

GHOST-BOY: Say what I say.

GOTH-GIRL: 4 A.M. knows all my secrets.

GHOST-BOY: Can I know your secrets?

> *(She cuts him.)*
>
> OW.

GOTH-GIRL: 4 A.M.'s when my dreams die.

GHOST-BOY: 4 A.M.'s when my dreams die.

> *(She cuts herself so she bleeds.)*

GHOST-BOY: Shit, you're serious.

> *(Goth-Girl says the following as Ghost-Boy echoes her.)*

GOTH-GIRL: *(Ghost-Boy echoes her.)* Cut me, change me, rearrange me, your blood is my blood, my blood is your blood, supernaturally, eternally, mix with me internally, change me irreversibly, effect me, infect me, fate me, alter me, lose time, find mine, let me be your land mine, 4 A.M. knows all my secrets, 4 A.M.'s when my dreams die. Drink me.

> *(She drinks his blood.)*

GOTH-GIRL: You're not safe with me.

GHOST-BOY: That's what I like about you.

> You're getting blood all over my shirt.

GOTH-GIRL: Take it off. Suck.

END OF SCENE

Scenes for Two Men

Almost, Maine
John Cariani

Comic
Chad and Randy, twenties to thirties

> *Chad and Randy are two country boys living in rural Maine. They
> are hanging out in a potato field, drinking some beers.*
>
> *Note on symbols: The next character to speak should begin his
> or her line where the // appears in the speech of the character speak-
> ing. The symbol > appears at the end of a line that is not a com-
> plete thought. It means that the character speaking should drive
> through to the end of the thought, which will be continued in his
> or her next lines. Don't stop for the other character's line.*

CHAD: I believe you, I'm just sayin' —

RANDY: It was bad, Chad. Bad.

CHAD: I hear ya, but —

RANDY: *(On "but":)* But you're not listenin', // Chad: It was bad! >

CHAD: No, *you're* not listenin', 'cause >

RANDY: Real bad.

CHAD: *(Topping Randy.)* I'm tryin' to tell you that I had a pretty bad time
    myself!!!

RANDY: *(Taking this in.)* No. There's no way! —

CHAD: It was pretty bad, Randy.

RANDY: Really?

CHAD: Yeah.

RANDY: OK: go.

CHAD: *(This is a little painful.)* She — . . . She said she didn't like the way
    I smelled.

RANDY: What?

CHAD: Sally told me she didn't like the way I smelled. Never has.

RANDY: *(Taking this in.)* Sally Dunleavy told you that she didn't // like —?

CHAD: Yeah.

RANDY: When?

CHAD: When I picked her up. She got in the truck, we were backin' outta her driveway, and all of a sudden, she started breathin' hard and asked me to stop and she got outta the truck and said she was sorry but she couldn't go out with me because she didn't like the way I smelled, never had! >

RANDY: What?

CHAD: Said she thought she was gonna be able to overlook it, the way that I smelled, but that that wasn't gonna be possible after all, and she slammed the door on me and left me sittin' right there in her driveway.

RANDY: *(Taking this in.)* 'Cause she didn't like the way you smelled?

CHAD: Yeah.

RANDY: Well what kinda — *(Beat.)* I don't mind the way you smell.

CHAD: Thanks.

RANDY: Jeez.

CHAD: Yeah . . . *(Beat.)* Told you it was bad.

RANDY: More than bad, Chad. That's sad.

CHAD: Yeah. *(Beat.)* So, I'm guessin' I'm the big winner tonight, huh? So . . . I get to pick tomorrow, and I pick bowlin'. We'll go bowlin', supper at the snowmobile club . . . coupla beers at the Moose Paddy . . . and just hang out.

RANDY: *(Looks at Chad.)* I didn't say you're the big winner, >

CHAD: What?

RANDY: did I say you're the big winner?

CHAD: No —

RANDY: No. All that's pretty sad, Chad, and bad, but you didn't win.

CHAD: What do you mean?

RANDY: You didn't win.

CHAD: You can beat bein' told you smelled bad?

RANDY: Yeah.

CHAD: Well then: *(i.e., "Let's hear it!")*

RANDY: Mine's face broke.

CHAD: What?

RANDY: Her face broke.

CHAD: *(Taking this in.)* Her —

RANDY: Only get one chance with a girl like Yvonne LaFrance, *(LaFrance rhymes with* pants.*)* and her face broke. *(Beat.)* Told you it was bad. *(Beat.)*

CHAD: *(Trying to figure out this broken face thing.)* How did her face break?

RANDY: When we were dancin'.

CHAD: *Dancin'? (i.e., Guys don't dance.)*

RANDY: Yup.

CHAD: Why were you dancin'?

RANDY: 'Cause that's what she wanted to do. On our date. So I took her. Took her dancin' down to the rec center. You pay, then you get a lesson, then you dance all night. They teach "together dancing," how to dance together, and we learned that thing where you throw the girl up and over, and, Yvonne — well, she's pretty small . . . and I'm pretty strong. And I threw her up and over, and, well . . . I threw her . . . *over* . . . over. *(Beat.)* And she landed on her face. *(Beat.)* And it broke. *(Beat.)* Had to take her to the emergency room. *(Beat.)*

CHAD: That's a drive.

RANDY: Thirty-eight miles.

CHAD: Yup.

(Beat.)

RANDY: *(Disgusted.)* And she cried.

CHAD: Hate that.

RANDY: Whole way.

(Beat.)

RANDY: Then had me call her old boyfriend to come get her.

CHAD: Ooh.

RANDY: He did. Asked me to "please leave."

(Beat.)

RANDY: He's small as she is.

(They laugh. Beat. Chad laughs.)

RANDY: What?

CHAD: That's just — pretty bad.

RANDY: Yup.

CHAD: And sad.

RANDY: Yup.

CHAD: So . . . I guess you win.

RANDY: Yup.

CHAD: That right here might make you the big winner of all time.

RANDY: Yup.

CHAD: "Baddest-date-guy" of all time.

RANDY: Yup.

CHAD: Congratulations.

RANDY: Thank you.

CHAD: So what do you pick tomorrow?

RANDY: Bowlin'. Supper at the snowmobile club. Coupla beers at the Moose Paddy. Hang out.

CHAD: Good.

(Beat. They drink their beers, which they finish and then throw offstage right into a potato barrel, maybe, like they're shooting baskets. Chad laughs.)

RANDY: What?

CHAD: I don't know. Just sometimes . . . I don't know why I bother goin' "out." I don't like it, Randy. I hate it. I hate goin' out on these dates. I mean, why do I wanna spend my Friday night with some girl I *might maybe* like, when I could be spendin' it hangin' out with someone I *know* I like, like you, you know?

RANDY: Yeah.

CHAD: I mean . . . that was rough tonight. In the middle of Sally tellin' me how she didn't like the way I smelled . . . I got real sad, >

RANDY: Aw. buddy —

CHAD: and all I could think about was how not much in this world makes me feel good or makes much sense anymore, and I got really scared 'cause there's gotta be something that makes you feel good or at least makes sense in this world, or what's the point, right?, and, then I kinda came out of bein' sad, and actually felt OK, 'cause I realized that there *is* one thing in this world that makes me feel really good and that *does* make sense, and it's you.

(Everything stops. Chad isn't quite sure what he has just said. Randy isn't quite sure what he has just heard. Long beat of these guys sorting out what was said and heard.)

RANDY: *(Quickly getting up to escape the discomfort.)* Well, I'm gonna head. *(He starts to leave.)* >

CHAD: Yeah . . .

RANDY: I gotta work in the mornin' . . .

CHAD: Well, I'm just supervising first shift at the mill, so I can pick you up anytime after 3 —

RANDY: Oh, I don't know, Chad: Me and Lendall, we got a lotta roofs to fix from all the snow in December.

CHAD: Well, 4 // or 5?

RANDY: Could take all day, I don't know when we'll be // done.

CHAD: Well, you just // say when —

RANDY: I don't know, I don't know, so, >

CHAD: Well —

RANDY: hey: I'll see ya later . . . *(Leaving.)*

CHAD: Yeah, yeah, yeah . . .

    (Chad watches Randy go. Then:)

CHAD: Hey, Randy —

    (Suddenly, Chad completely falls on the ground. Love is, after all, often described as making people "weak in the knees.")

RANDY: *(Turning, seeing Chad on the ground.)* Whoah! Chad! You OK?

CHAD: Yeah . . .

RANDY: What the — . . . Here . . . *(Helping Chad up.)*

CHAD: Thanks. Umm . . .

RANDY: What was that? You OK? What just happened there?

CHAD: *(Trying to figure this out.)* Umm . . . I just fell . . .

RANDY: Well, I figured that out . . .

CHAD: No *(i.e., it's more than that.)* . . . I just — . I think I just fell in love with you there, Randy.

RANDY: *(Silence.)*

    (Chad looks at Randy, then suddenly and completely falls down again.)

RANDY/CHAD: Ho!

CHAD: *(On the ground.)* Yup. That's what that was. *(Getting up.)* Me falling in love with you . . . *(He falls down again, suddenly and completely.)*

RANDY: Chad: What are you doin'? Come on, get up! *(Randy gets Chad up, roughly.)*

CHAD: Randy —

(Randy helps Chad up again; Chad immediately falls down again.)

CHAD: Whoah!

RANDY: *(Fiercely.)* Would you cut that out!

CHAD: *(Fiercely, right back.)* Well, I can't help it!! It just kinda came over me! I've fallen in love with you, here!

(Randy takes this in. He is not happy. FEAR. Long beat.)

RANDY: Chad: I'm your best buddy in the whole world . . . and I don't quite know what you're doin' or what you're goin' on about . . . but *(Angry.)* — what the heck is your problem? What the heck are you doin'? Jeezum Crow, you're my best friend, >

CHAD: Yeah —

RANDY: and that's — . . . That's a thing you don't mess with. And you messed with it. And you don't do that. *(He starts to go. Then, fiercely:)* 'Cause, you know somethin', you're about the only thing that feels really good and makes sense in this world to me, too, and then you go and foul it up, and now it just doesn't make any sense at all. And it doesn't feel good. *(Starts to leave again.)* You've done a real number on a good thing, here, buddy, 'cause we're friends, and there's a line, when you're friends, *(Turning back to Chad.)* that you can't cross. And you crossed it. *(Randy is now on the opposite side of the stage from Randy, and he suddenly and completely falls down. He is on the opposite side of the stage from Chad. Randy and Chad just stare at each other. They are far away from each other. Chad points to Randy, asking nonverbally if the same thing just happened to him. Randy nods. This is about as scary and wonderful as it gets. A moment of realization. Music. Lights fade.)*

END OF SCENE

Are We There Yet?
Garth Wingfield

Comic
Moss, early thirties or younger; Julian, early thirties or younger

> *This scene is from early in the play and gives us a sense of Moss's dating life (it's not good).*

> *(Moss and Julian dance in, carrying chairs that they arrange to suggest a table in a restaurant. A song plays under and out.)*

MOSS: This place is unbelievable!

JULIAN: Isn't it wild, Moss?

MOSS: How did you find it?

JULIAN: We've been coming here forever.

MOSS: There are literally Chianti bottles with candles in this restaurant. It's like 1955 in here!

JULIAN: We think so too. And the food's amazing.

MOSS: Really?

JULIAN: Well, very *severe* Italian. Now, you are going to have to swear to me you will only bring your dearest friends here. Word must not get out.

MOSS: OK . . .

JULIAN: No! Look me in the eyes. Swear to me, Moss. Nothing would send my life into a tailspin more than having the *Times'* "$25 and Under" column finding out about this.

MOSS: *(Little smile.)* Fine. I swear.

JULIAN: God, you're adorable. I totally want to kiss you.

MOSS: *(Weakening.)* Rosemary Clooney *is* encouraging us . . .
  (Julian kisses Moss fast.)

JULIAN: You have no idea how much I've wanted to do that for the past three months.

MOSS: It's been that long?

JULIAN: June 13th was the first time we saw each other. Not that I'm counting.

MOSS: Weeks and weeks of making gay eyes at one another on the subway platform on the way to work . . .

JULIAN: *Praying* the train won't come . . .

MOSS: I was so relieved when you finally said something the other day.

JULIAN: I've had major fantasies about you, fella. Like I bet you're a decorator.

MOSS: *(His hackles up a bit.)* Really? I come off like a decorator?

JULIAN: Sure, I thought so.

MOSS: How? My hair, or . . . ?

JULIAN: You wear Calvin Klein's Obsession *a lot.*

MOSS: God, I had no idea I was sending that signal. *(Then.)* I'm an editor at a publishing house.

JULIAN: Impressive.

MOSS: Please, it's stupid. There's a seamy, soul-draining side to the whole affair. I thought it'd be glamorous, too. I pictured myself editing Anne Tyler and Joyce Carol Oates. Instead, I just edited the *Coopers & Lybrand Tax Guide.*

But. What do *you* do?

JULIAN: What's your little fantasy of my life?

MOSS: *(Flirty smile.)* Well, I . . . I've fully convinced myself that you're a surgeon.

JULIAN: Really?

MOSS: And you specialize in pediatrics.

JULIAN: Huh.

MOSS: I mean, you have nice fingers, and you seem so gentle.

JULIAN: That's very sweet.

MOSS: But I'm . . . guessing I'm wrong . . .

JULIAN: Sort of.

I'm a decorator.

(Little beat.)

MOSS: Uh-huh . . .

JULIAN: Mostly high-end stuff on the Upper East Side. Let's just say I'm not afraid of chintz.

MOSS: *(Pulling in.)* That's . . . I never would've guessed decorator. *(Off his menu.)* So what's good?

JULIAN: Well, we always have the penne with mushrooms. And we love the calamari.

MOSS: "We?"

JULIAN: What?

MOSS: You've been saying "we."

JULIAN: Have I?

MOSS: Constantly.

JULIAN: Really?

MOSS: I really can't help but wonder, Who's "we"? Your friends and all, or . . . ?

JULIAN: No, my boyfriend.

MOSS: I'm sorry?

JULIAN: Hector. I told you about him.

MOSS: No, you didn't.

JULIAN: Sure, I did. You know, that time I called you?

MOSS: No, Julian. No, you didn't. You mentioned nothing of this Hector person, who you're what . . .

JULIAN: Living with, uh-huh.

MOSS: I was going to say . . . actually, I was hoping *you* would say "breaking up with" . . .

JULIAN: No, things are fine with us. But you're a total stud. And he works late *a lot.*

MOSS: I'm sorry, Julian, but this isn't what I'd hoped for.

JULIAN: What's wrong.

MOSS: I've gotta go.

JULIAN: What are you talking about? We're here. In 1955! We're having dinner.

MOSS: I thought we were having a date!

JULIAN: *We are!*

MOSS: *(To audience.)* And that's when I threw a glass of wine in his face. *(Julian stands.)*

JULIAN: I cannot believe you just did that! I'll have you know I'm wearing a brand-new Banana Republic shirt here. That I'd bought just for you. Red wine! Vicious!

(He goes. Moss stands there for a sec.)

END OF SCENE

Cowboy Versus Samurai
Michael Golamco

Comic
Travis and Chester, both twenties to thirties

> *Travis and Chester are the only two Asian Americans in a small
> Wyoming town. Chester is the president of the town's "Asian-
> American Alliance." Travis is the group's only other member. Here,
> they are having a meeting.*

*(A small-town high school classroom. Travis Park sits alone in one of the
student desk chairs. He's doodling on a piece of paper. Chester stands at
a teacher's desk. He is possibly dressed in black military fatigues, Che
Guevarran. He bangs a gavel —)*

CHESTER: Order! As president of the Breakneck Asian American Alliance,
I call this meeting to order! Will the secretary rise and read the minutes from our last meeting?

(Travis stands, flips the piece of paper over and reads off of it —)

TRAVIS: Last week we discussed the fact that Shelby's Grocery Store
doesn't carry tofu. Then we discussed boycotting Shelby's Grocery
Store. Then our president attempted to find a method for ordering
tofu through the Internet . . . And then the secretary called the president a moron.

CHESTER: Moving on —

TRAVIS: And then we voted on whether the president actually is a moron,
which ended in a tie —

CHESTER: Yes, MOVING ON. Our first order of business is —

(Travis raises his hand —)

CHESTER: Yes.

TRAVIS: I move that we change our regular meeting place to Heck's Tavern.

CHESTER: Anyone second that motion?

(Travis sighs and raises his hand again.)

CHESTER: All right, let's bring it to a vote. All in favor, say "AYE."

TRAVIS: Aye.

CHESTER: All opposed say "NAY." Nay. All right, we have a tie. In which case, the bylaws of BAAA state that the president must make a final decision . . . And his decision is: NO.

TRAVIS: Oh come on, Chester! If I have to come to these stupid meetings I want to be able to drink a beer.

CHESTER: In order to preserve BAAA's integrity, BAAA must maintain meeting locations that do not serve alcohol.

TRAVIS: Would you quit saying "BAAA"? You sound like a militant sheep.

CHESTER: I am anything but sheep-like, my Brother. The Asian Man must stand for dignity and righteousness — not getting red-in-the-face while he falls off a bar stool.

TRAVIS: These meetings are a joke. You and I are the only Asian people in town.

CHESTER: Which is why we must maintain Solidarity, my Korean Brother. Solidarity in the face of constant and deliberate oppression. Shelby's Grocery Store: an openly racist seller of Occidental-only foodstuffs.

TRAVIS: Mr. Shelby has said, repeatedly, that he won't carry anything that only two people are going to buy.

CHESTER: Solidarity. Heck's Tavern: Center of Foreign and Domestic Imperialism, what with its so-called selection of "Import Beer." Where's my Tsing-Tao? My Kirin Ichiban? Can I get a fuckin' Hite?

TRAVIS: I thought you weren't into getting red-faced and falling off bar stools.

CHESTER: Well I might be if I could get a glass of something from the Motherland. See, Travis, one voice alone accomplishes nothing. And that's why BAAA exists — to give us more than one voice.

TRAVIS: Two voices.

CHESTER: That's right: Two Strong Asian-American voices. And if you and I stick together, we can affect some change in this shitty little town.

TRAVIS: But you see Chester, I like this shitty little town. I like the fact that Heck hasn't changed his tavern since 1973. I like —

CHESTER: Well —

TRAVIS: Shut up. I like bowling in a two-lane alley that's connected to an Episcopal Church. I like flipping through the library's *National*

Geographics with all the aboriginal titties snipped out. I like all of these things because I enjoy certain charms. The charms, if you will, of small-town life. And I know you grew up here, but these things are still new to me.

CHESTER: If I had a car and some money, I'd be sipping iced green tea on a beach. But that's OK. Don't lift a finger, remain seated in your little Caucasian corner. I will handle this week's business by myself: the BAAA membership drive.

TRAVIS: Membership drive?

CHESTER: Yes. There's a potential new member moving into town. Last name Lee.

TRAVIS: There are plenty of Lees that aren't Asian. Christopher Lee. Tommy Lee Jones. Lee Majors.

CHESTER: From New York.

TRAVIS: Spike Lee.

CHESTER: From Flushing Queens.

TRAVIS: Flushing what?

CHESTER: You're from California, so you wouldn't understand. Flushing, Queens is the Korean capital of New York City. And it gets better: last name Lee, first name Veronica.
(Deliciously.)
Korean Veronica Lee.

TRAVIS: Leave her alone, Chester. Keep your crazy militant shit to yourself.

CHESTER: No way fella. It's bad enough living in this two-donkey town. I'm an island of yellow in a sea of white.

TRAVIS: It's like someone took a piss in the snow.

CHESTER: We are going to embrace this hopefully lovely Korean Sister with open arms and show her that Asian America thrives in Breakneck, Wyoming. You actually have another thing in common with her: She's also a teacher.

TRAVIS: Wonderful. Now we know you won't be able to hypnotize her into drinking your Kool-Aid.

CHESTER: You always belittle my ideas, Travis. Why is that?

TRAVIS: It's because your ideas are stupid, Chester. If you tell her your conspiracy theory that American rice contains penis-shrinking chemicals, I'm walking out.

CHESTER: I am upholding our identity, my brother. For within that identity lies our dignity.

TRAVIS: Fine. But give it a rest sometime, OK? Support some other causes. Save the Whales. Stop deforestation. Become a Nazi or something.
(As he exits —)

TRAVIS: And one more thing — next time I'm going to be at Heck's Tavern, with or without you. I might even start my own club. The Breakneck Travis American Alliance. That's B-TAAH to you. B-TAAH! Anyone who wants to drink beer with me is in. Make it the Breakneck Beer American Alliance. Buh-buh-Ahh! Buh-buh-Ahh!
(Travis exits.)
(Chester in prayer:)

CHESTER: O Bruce, please show Travis the error of his ways. He's a good guy, even if he is a race traitor. Oh, and by the way, please make sure that Veronica Lee is hot. Hot-and-buttered. Shie-shie, O Great One.
(He bows.)

END OF SCENE

Cowboy Versus Samurai
Michael Golamco

Comic

Travis and Del, late twenties to early thirties; Travis is an Asian-American

Travis and Del live in a small town in Wyoming, where Travis teaches school. His friend Del is a cowboy, in love with the only Asian-American woman in town. Travis fancies her, too — but she only dates white guys. Here, while playing catch, Del asks Travis to write his lady love a love letter. Shades of Cyrano de Bergerac!

(Outdoors. Dusk. Sound of crickets chirping, a light wind, the hum of a faraway freeway. Del stands at the side, kneading his glove. Travis is on the opposite side, also wearing a baseball glove. Travis pitches an invisible ball at Del, who catches it.)

DEL: *(Reciting from memory and often messing up.)* Ladies and gentlemen, welcome to Cheyenne Pete's Wild West Show and Indoor Rodeo —

TRAVIS: *(Coaching him through.)* Yee-haw. Don't forget the yee-haw, it's important —
(They pitch the ball back and forth, playing catch —)

DEL: Right. Yee-haw. I am Cheyenne Pete, your head honcho for this evening's . . .

TRAVIS: Entertainment —

DEL: Entertainment; you are about to witness the most earth-shaking —

TRAVIS: Earthshaking-est —

DEL: Earthshaking-est, most breathtaking buffalo —

TRAVIS: Breathtaking-est —

DEL: God damn — Breathtaking-est buffalo and bronco blowout . . . Uh . . .

TRAVIS: *(Finishing it.)* This side of the Mississippi. We got Figure-Eight trick ropers, we got Ornery Owen the Horn-Ed steer — but don't you worry 'cause the arena you see before you is TRIPLE

REINFORCED — and if you'd like an autograph from a real live Indian, please ask your server. Now, get ready to cheer for your section's cowboy, 'cause Cheyenne Pete's Wild West Show has just begun. Yee-haw . . .

You were supposed to have that memorized.

DEL: Hold on.

(He produces a half-smoked joint, lights it, takes a long drag —)

DEL: OK. From the top.

TRAVIS: Is that a joint?

DEL: It helps me remember things. Gets me relaxed. I get a little stoned, go over what I need to know, and when it comes time to repeat the information, I get stoned again and it comes right back to me.

TRAVIS: So you were stoned when you were memorizing your lines?

DEL: No. But I am now relaxed.

TRAVIS: You shouldn't be smoking weed, Del. You're a teacher for christ's sake.

DEL: I'm a P. E. teacher. And this isn't even my weed. It's Bill's weed. So if I ever get caught smoking it, I'll just say, "Dad, Sir, this is not my weed. It's Bill's. I found it in his room — see, he buys it from a quarter-Indian dealer named Mystery Dream. So as you can see, Sir, Bill is just as much of a hucklefuck as your other son. Me."

TRAVIS: That's good, that'll show him. You want to work on your audition now?

DEL: I don't wanna audition for Cheyenne Pete's anymore, Travis. That speech was probably written by a Texan.

TRAVIS: You can't move off of your dad's ranch on a part-time P. E. teacher's salary.

DEL: I know.

TRAVIS: So what are you going to do?

DEL: Man, I dunno.

(He pinches out the joint and sticks it in his mouth. He puts his glove back on.)

DEL: Toss me the ball.

(The game of catch resumes.)

DEL: You met the new teacher?

TRAVIS: Veronica? Yeah.

DEL: She's from New York City, Travis. New York City.

TRAVIS: You've talked to her?

DEL: Aww . . . Naw, man. I wouldn't know what to say. She's different.

TRAVIS: What do you mean, different?

DEL: She's not like the girls around here, not like the girls on TV . . . She's Ko-rean, right? Hooo — I didn't expect a Ko-rean girl to look like that.

TRAVIS: What did you think they looked like?

DEL: I dunno. Like you in a wig?

(Travis pitches a fastball that slams, hard, into Del's mitt. Del notices the extra heat on it —)

DEL: Ow . . . What?

TRAVIS: It's funny how a beautiful woman transcends all racial boundaries.

DEL: What's that?

TRAVIS: A beautiful Asian woman moves into town and you're biting your fist at how fine she is. But when I moved in? "Hey Jap! Go back to China!"

DEL: So you're still holding that over my head.

TRAVIS: I just think it's funny, that's all.

DEL: I didn't know you back then. I thought you were a tourist. I didn't even know you could speak English.

TRAVIS: I'm touched.

DEL: Yeap, I'm in-the-know now. I'm sensitive to things.

(Del begins to quietly chant her name as he winds up and pitches —)

DEL: Verrr-onica . . . Lee-lee-lee-lee . . .

TRAVIS: You really like her.

DEL: Why'dya say that?

TRAVIS: You're doing that lee-lee-lee-lee thing.

DEL: She's pretty.

TRAVIS: Why don't you introduce yourself?

DEL: I sorta already tried.

TRAVIS: And?

DEL: I saw her in your classroom at the beginning of lunch. And I dunno, I just kind of stood in the doorway for a little while trying to think of something to say. But she just looked so damn professional, y'know? And before I could speak up, she said, "Hey — you gotta mop up a bit more around the door 'cause one of the kids threw up during first period. And also please empty the trash on your way out 'cause you forgot to do it last night. Thanks." And when I got back from emptying out the trash, she was gone. Which is good, I guess, 'cause on the way to the dumpster I was rackin' my brain for something to say and I couldn't think of nothin'.

TRAVIS: What's the problem? You don't have any trouble talking to other women.

DEL: I know the girls around here. We got a common thing going. But not Veronica. She's got that big city get-the-hell-outta-my-way thing going on . . . And she's Ko-rean.

TRAVIS: So what if she's Ko-rean? She's just like everybody else. The only difference between us and her is that she's fine as hell.

DEL: I know. It messes up my train of thought.

So I was gonna ask you if maybe you could help me out.

TRAVIS: What am I supposed to do?

DEL: You lived in a big city. And, you're Ko-rean too — you don't know what it's like living here all your life. You've been other places, seen things.

TRAVIS: So what?

DEL: My whole life it's been the same stuff. The same people. And I want something different.

TRAVIS: Why don't you write her a note or something?

DEL: Yeah! What?

TRAVIS: A note: a nonverbal communication written on a piece of paper —

DEL: I know what a note is, Travis. I've written 'em many times to myself.

TRAVIS: So go. Activate.

DEL: But what's it supposed to say?

TRAVIS: Everything you just said to me right now sounds pretty good.

DEL: No it doesn't. It don't sound good, Travis. You gotta make it sound good, see? And you — you're good with words — I always see you readin' some book or other —

TRAVIS: Sure.

DEL: You're good at communicating with people, Travis. You're an English teacher — your job is to put words together —

TRAVIS: No. My job is to give kids books so they can draw penises in the margins.

DEL: All I need is a little cheat-sheet or something. Write something for me.

TRAVIS: Get off me.

DEL: Come on Travis. Please.

TRAVIS: I don't even know if it'll do any good. She says that she's intent on being single.

DEL: But why not give it a shot? "Stories are powerful" — that's what you say. So maybe write me a little story.

(A pause as Travis considers this.)

TRAVIS: All right.

DEL: *(Elated.)* Thanks Travis. I owe you, man.

TRAVIS: No more weed. That's my asking price.

DEL: Done.

(He makes a grand ceremonial gesture of tossing the joint away.)

DEL: By the way, I'm sorry I called you a Jap before.

TRAVIS: It's OK. I get it all the time.

(They continue to play catch.)

END OF SCENE

Cyclone
Ron Fitzgerald

Dramatic
Bob, early twenties; Mitch, late twenties to early thirties

> *This is the opening scene of the play. Bob works in a convenience store. A possibly dangerous customer named Mitch comes in late one night, carrying a mysterious paper cup.*

> *(Late night. A small convenience store in a remote part of the vast New Jersey wasteland. A clerk with "Bob" stitched on his shirt is at the register, looking deeply into an extremely large cup. Mitch is opposite the clerk, ripping open a fresh pack of Camel Lights. A small box sits at his feet.)*

BOB: What's this?

MITCH: A fucking cup.

BOB: It's empty.

MITCH: I just want the cup.

BOB: But I still got to charge you for the soda.

MITCH: I don't want the soda. I just want the fucking cup.

BOB: But I still got to charge you.

MITCH: I don't want any Ring Dings either, you want to charge me for those?

BOB: We don't have Ring Dings. I can charge you for Ho-Hos.

MITCH: I'm not really in the mood to be fucked with, OK there um . . . Bob.

BOB: Bob's not here now.

MITCH: Bob's not . . . What the fuck are you talking about? It says Bob on your shirt.

BOB: I'm talking about Bob's not here 'cause he went to the Poconos. To see the stock car races. That's why I'm here. I'm here 'cause Bob's not. 'Cause he went to the Poconos.

MITCH: To see the stock car races.

BOB: Bob really likes those races.

MITCH: Can I have my cup now?

BOB: My name's Bob too. But I'm not *the Bob*. Not the Bob who works here. I'm the *other Bob*. The Bob that works at the paint store. I mix paint. I mix a lot of paint. All day. All different colors. You know? Paints. Mixed. Together. That's what I do.

MITCH: Bob?

BOB: Yes?

MITCH: Can I have my fucking cup please?

BOB: Just the cup?

MITCH: Just the cup.

BOB: But I still gotta charge you for —

MITCH: I know.

BOB: You sure you don't want the soda?

MITCH: I'm fucking positive.

BOB: People usually get the beverage with that.

MITCH: I guess I'm living on the edge.

(Mitch lights a cigarette.)

BOB: Hey, ummm . . . You can't like smoke in here.

MITCH: Sure I can. It's easy. See?

BOB: No, I mean, you're not *allowed* to smoke in here. Store policy.

MITCH: I'm just going to smoke a little.

BOB: Yeah, but . . .

MITCH: Relax. It's just me and you. Out here in the middle of buttfuck nowhere.

BOB: Are you lost or something?

MITCH: Hell no. I've been looking for this place.

Well, not this place. I was really looking for this other place. But here I am anyway. Like I was just driving around, looking for this shithole the whole time.

BOB: It's actually nicer when the sun's up.

(Mitch puts his cigarette out on the floor.)

MITCH: I'll bet it just glows.

(Mitch takes the bag of ashes from the box and pours them into the cup.)

MITCH: You like your job Bob? I mean . . . you like working here . . . this little life you got going? You a uhh . . . *people* person?

BOB: People tend to avoid me.

MITCH: I hate them. People. Jobs. You name it. I just don't . . . I just don't like them. Assholes and work. That's all there is.

BOB: You gotta pay the bills.

MITCH: Yes you do. You always got to pay somebody for something.

I guess it's kinda like cigarettes. Huh? A chunk of genuine nastiness, but you get used to it. At some point you even get addicted. The shit gets beyond your control and you're just flying on autopilot. You know what I mean?

BOB: I don't smoke.

MITCH: Then I guess you don't know what I mean.

BOB: It's not that I don't want to smoke. It's just . . . you're not allowed to in here.

MITCH: Yeah, you mentioned that.

BOB: And at home . . . my folks don't want me to . . . and the car would smell and . . . I don't really want to listen to them bitching at me, so . . .

MITCH: Yeah.

BOB: . . . so . . . which is fucked, you know? Because they both smoke.

MITCH: People are definitely fucked.

BOB: Yeah.

MITCH: Look at you.

BOB: Me?

MITCH: Fucking little pissant clerk who's afraid to have a smoke when he wants one. I'd say that's pretty fucked.

BOB: I'm not afraid. I just . . . I don't want to poison my body with that shit. I'm not afraid.

MITCH: Sure.

BOB: I'm not. I got a tattoo.

MITCH: Yeah?

BOB: It's very cool. It hurt like hell. It's the Keltic symbol for strength and courage and . . . I think the pope or something.

MITCH: Let's see it.

BOB: It's not really . . . *accessible* . . . right now.

MITCH: Right.

You know what's in this cup? You know what I got in here?

BOB: No.

MITCH: Take a guess.

BOB: Dirt?

MITCH: Dirt. Close. My father . . . My dad . . . is in this cup . . . his . . . his *ashes* are in this cup. Sixty-four ounces of Dad. Right here.

BOB: Oh.

MITCH: More restive than the shoe box, don't you think?

BOB: Did you say . . . your dad?

MITCH: Yeah.

BOB: Wow. My dad's at home.

MITCH: You ever wish he was dead?

BOB: No.

MITCH: Why not?

BOB: I don't know. He's my dad.

MITCH: Yeah. Course.

> *(Mitch picks up the cup of ashes.)*

> Look at this thing. If this was Coke or Pepsi . . . it would be too much, right? Who could drink it all? It's a fucking bucket.

> But it's just my dad. It doesn't seem like enough. It's not very big, I mean, he was a pretty big guy, you know . . . and now . . . look how little there is . . . I mean . . . after everything and all . . . and now there's just . . . he fit in this *fucking cup* for chrissake.

> *(Mitch slams the cup down. A puff of ash escapes. Bob watches as it settles on the counter.)*

BOB: Do you want like a . . . a lid for that?

MITCH: You want to hear something funny? My dad was a cop. Got killed in a shitty store just like this. Walked in on a robbery and . . . BLAM! . . . that was that. You go in for a pack of cigarettes and you get smoked. That's kind of funny, don't you think?

BOB: I guess.

MITCH: And now here we are. I mean . . . if I was robbing this place right now, someone's dad could walk through that door, and I could just shoot him. I guess that's kinda funny too.

BOB: Yeah.

MITCH: The best is . . . this place . . . this shitty place. With the gasoline. And the cigarettes. And my dad. This is perfect. It just about feels

like home. How funny is that? I mean . . . how funny is . . . How
funny is that?

BOB: I'm not sure.

MITCH: You ever think about death, Bob?

BOB: Death?

MITCH: The opposite of life. You ever think about it?

BOB: Sometimes I guess. Like when I listen to Metallica.

MITCH: How about right now?

BOB: Now?

MITCH: Do you think death is part of some circle? Some circle of life bullshit? Or do you think maybe it's punishment for something you did?
Something bad?

BOB: I don't know. I'm not really thinking about it right now.
(Mitch pulls a gun. He points it at Bob's head.)

MITCH: How about now? I bet you're thinking about it now.
(Bob stares into the dark barrel of the gun.)

END OF SCENE

Cyclone
Ron Fitzgerald

Dramatic
Bob, early twenties; Mitch, late twenties to early thirties

> *Bob, a clerk in a convenience store, comes over to the trailer park*
> *where a demented customer named Mitch lives. Bob wants to know*
> *why Mitch shot him.*

> *(Just before dawn. Mitch and Erin's yard looks pretty much the same*
> *except for the Flamingo that is, perhaps, a bit yellower. Mitch staggers*
> *in and slumps on the steps. He is carrying a six-pack of Pabst and the*
> *charred, twisted, and partially melted cup of ashes. He sets them on the*
> *stairs and lights a smoke. After a moment Bob walks in holding his arm,*
> *which is wrapped in a bloody American flag.)*

BOB: You shot me.

MITCH: You want a beer?

BOB: You shot me.

MITCH: You keep saying that.

BOB: I've never been shot before.

MITCH: Do you want a beer or not?

BOB: I want to go to the hospital.

MITCH: For what?

BOB: You shot me.

MITCH: I didn't shoot you much, Bob. I mean . . . it was just one time
    for Christ's sake.

BOB: I lost a lot of blood.

MITCH: It's just a little hole.

BOB: I feel kinda dizzy.

MITCH: Why don't you have a nice beer? Beer is good for gunshot wounds.

BOB: I've been bleeding for a long time. I mean, I was bleeding in the car
    and . . . in the parking lot . . . and at the store. I've been bleeding

for hours because you shot me at like . . . like . . . What time do you think you shot me?

MITCH: I'm not really sure.

BOB: It was dark out. I remember that. Do you remember that?

MITCH: Yeah.

BOB: Well it gets dark around . . . around . . . What time do you think it gets dark?

MITCH: I have no idea.

BOB: OK, but like *around?*

MITCH: It gets dark around my nineteenth beer.

BOB: I'm a dead man.

MITCH: No, you'll be fine.

BOB: I should just start digging a hole.

MITCH: You're not going to bleed to death, Bob. I only shot you a little bit. And we've got you nice and wrapped up there.

BOB: You promise?

MITCH: Yeah. I promise.

BOB: OK. You know, you did a good job here with this thing. My arm. It's very . . . you know . . . *wrapped* . . . and all. If it wasn't that I was shot, it would be . . . I don't know . . . sort of . . . Cool. 'Cause it's nice material.

MITCH: Consider it a gift.

BOB: Hey thanks.

(Bob takes in the yard.)

You know this is . . . kinda nice here. You got a yard . . . sort of . . . and you know . . . some steps . . . and . . . hey, you got a pelican there, huh?

MITCH: It's a flamingo.

BOB: A flamingo? Why is it yellow?

MITCH: It's molting.

BOB: Weird.

(Bob picks up the baseball glove.)

Baseball. You got a kid or something?

MITCH: It's mine.

(Bob slips the glove on his good hand.)

BOB: Kinda small. You got a ball? We could play catch.

I guess that's stupid, huh? I mean, I can't really throw, can I? My arm's all fucked up. I can still catch though.

I sure do appreciate what you did for my arm here. I mean, the flag part, not the shooting part. Not that the shooting part's *bad* or anything . . . it's just . . . I would have got blood all over Bob's shirt, and then . . . he would have got back from the Poconos and been all like . . . *"Dude, you got fucking paint all over my shirt"* . . . and I would have had to go like *"Dude, it's not paint, it's my fucking blood"* . . . and then he would be all like *"Yeah. Right. What did you do, get another one of your nosebleeds?"* . . . and I'd be like *"No, Bob. I got, like, shot. Like while you were at the fucking Poconos watching a stupid fucking car race and drinking fucking beer and talking to fucking girls and watching a bunch of assholes drive around in a fucking circle, I was at the fucking store, Bob OK? I was at the fucking store, behind the fucking counter, in your fucking shirt, working your fucking shift, and getting fucking SHOT, Bob. So fuck you, Bob. FUCK YOU BOB YOU STUPID FUCK."*

He'd fucking shit . . . I said all that . . . he'd . . . he'd hide the coffee.

MITCH: OK, now I want to go to the hospital.

BOB: I'm really sorry I threw that water on your dad.

MITCH: That's OK.

BOB: Flame makes me kinda nervous.

MITCH: I noticed that.

BOB: It's all because of Bambi. That forest fire. Movie really messed me up.

MITCH: Let's go see the doctor. It'll be fun.

BOB: No, no . . . I'm all right.

MITCH: You don't seem all right.

BOB: I'm fine. I want a beer.

MITCH: What about your arm?

BOB: I can drink with this hand.

(Bob slurps a beer.)

MITCH: Look. I'm really sorry I shot you Bob.

BOB: No, it's cool. I got this amazing feeling all of a sudden. Like something in my head moved. Like at first, I thought it was all the blood . . . like I was dizzy almost. Like when I mix a lot of paint and I get all spaced out on the fumes. And sometimes I think I'm still mixing paint . . . when I'm not . . . I'm actually just sitting there. And then sometimes I think I'm just sitting there . . . and I'm not. I'm actually still mixing paint. So like now . . . now I think that I could be going home, or to the hospital, but actually I could be doing anything. I mean . . . I'm shot. I don't know where I am. I don't know what I'm doing. But I know I'm not mixing paint. And I know I'm not just sitting here. This isn't just some dream. This isn't just me being dizzy. This is . . . This is *this.*

MITCH: This is *what?*

BOB: This.

MITCH: This?

BOB: Yeah.

MITCH: What are you talking about?

BOB: You. Me. Your dad. The pelican. We're all part of *this.*

MITCH: *This* used to be a swamp, OK?

BOB: No, I get it now.

MITCH: You, me, my dad, the *flamingo* — we're standing on a heap of solid waste.

BOB: No, I see how things are. For real. This is . . . this is life.

MITCH: This is not life.

BOB: Of course it is.

MITCH: I fucking shot you Bob.

BOB: And I'm glad you did.

MITCH: I'm pretty sure that's insane.

BOB: Maybe you need to get shot.

Yeah. You see now that I've like . . . stared death in the face . . . and like looked into the abyss and shit . . . I'm no longer the normal Bob of old . . . you know *Old Bob.* No, no . . . Now, I'm like . . . like . . . like *New Bob,* you know? I'm like a laser . . . and like sharp . . . and, and . . . sharp and, and . . . ready to take charge and . . . and sharp.

MITCH: I can totally see that.

BOB: Fuck yeah!

MITCH: So, do you want another beer?

BOB: I want to go to Europe. I want to wear a backpack. I want to drink wine out of a skin.

MITCH: All I have is Pabst.

BOB: That's not enough for New Bob. New Bob is going to Paris.

(Bob suddenly looks four inches taller. Mitch raises his beer in salute.)

MITCH: Well. Bon voyage, New Bob.

BOB: Bon Voyage. Right on.

Bon Voyage.

What the hell's that mean?

END OF SCENE

Natural Selection
Eric Coble

Comic

Henry, thirties to forties; Man, twenties to thirties

> *Henry works for a vast theme park, in a future time, which seeks
> to preserve our lost heritage. He has been charged with finding a
> replacement North American, and he has gone off on an expedition
> to the American Southwest to find one. He has bagged this man from
> a helicopter with a tranquilizer dart, and he has brought him back
> to the theme park. The man, whose name it turns out is Zhao, is
> just waking up.*

> *(A traditional Navajo song starts quietly. Henry scoots a little bowl in
> front of the man, crouches a safe distance back from him.)*
> *(The man blinks his eyes — looks around . . . dazed . . .)*

HENRY: *(Quietly.)* It's OK. Um. "Dineh." "Ho' zho' ni'." Safe. You're safe.
   See?

> *(Holds up a little rug.)*
> Home? Safe at home?
> *(Beat. They stare at each other.)*

MAN: What the fuck is goin' on?

HENRY: What?

MAN: Why am I tied up? What're you doin', man? Get me loose! I want
   a lawyer — I didn't do nothin' —

HENRY: No. Oh no. No.

MAN: Where am I? Get those Goddamn pots away from me!
   (He kicks a bowl across the room.)

HENRY: No! Don't kick it! Don't break it! Those are genuine! They're part
   of your tribe! They're primitive! You're supposed to be primitive —
   You're a genuine Native American!! Native Americans don't break
   their own artifacts!

MAN: . . . what?

HENRY: Who are you?? What are you doing in my office?

MAN: I don't know! What am I doin' in your office?

HENRY: Tell me you're Navajo, please tell me you're Navajo —

MAN: What the hell you want to know for? I got rights. I can get a lawyer. You can't keep me here —

HENRY: Oh crap. Oh crap oh crap oh crap —

MAN: Untie me, man! I ain't done nothin'!

HENRY: OK. Listen. Just listen. Um. Are you Native American?

(Beat. The man looks at Henry.)

MAN: Navajo on my mother's side, asshole.

HENRY: Just your mother?

MAN: My dad's from Guadalajara.

HENRY: You're not even a full-blood.

MAN: What's that got to do with anything?

HENRY: You were herding sheep in the open desert! What the heck were you doing herding sheep in the open desert when you're only part Indian?

MAN: I was visiting my tia and tio on the Rez. They got sheep. Is that illegal now?

HENRY: Are your aunt and uncle full-bloods? Why am I even asking? The budget's gone. I just blew the budget!

MAN: I'm not talkin', 'til I get a lawyer.

HENRY: Darn it!

(Beat.)

Dammit!

(Henry stares at the man, who stares back. Long moments pass . . .)

(Henry taps his fingers on the desk lightly . . . Then . . .)

HENRY: *(Continued.)* You want something to drink? I can get you a Pepsi or something.

(Beat. The man stares at him.)

My treat.

(The man stares. More moments pass . . . Then Henry laughs.)

HENRY: *(Continued.)* Surprise! This is . . . ah . . .

(Begins untying the man.)

— it's a new promotion we're doing. To, ah, to get folks into the park. Get it? "It's so much fun, you'll have to be tied down!" My understanding is rope burns disappear very quickly. There shouldn't be any lasting . . . redness . . .

(The man sits up, now free. They look at each other.)

MAN: Where am I?

HENRY: WonderWorld, you idiot!! Sorry! Sorry! I just assumed — Hooo! Still a little tense. My first . . . first marketing foray. As it were. On behalf of everyone at Culture Fiesta, allow me to welcome you to the Happiest Place on Earth.

(At his desk.)

And we would like to offer you a five-day pass — all expenses paid — it's all on us — including airfare back to New Mexico. We already flew you here. What, ah, what name should I fill out on the paperwork? Benally? Begay? Yazzie?

MAN: Martinez.

HENRY: Of course. Mexican.

MAN: Zhao Martinez.

(Henry puts his head in his hands.)

ZHAO: Named for my grandpa. He was Chinese-Brazilian. Met my grandma in Jamaica.

(Henry slumps farther down on his desk.)

ZHAO: *(Continued.)* You shoot everyone you want to come to your park?

MAN: *(Shoves a paper across the desk.)* I'm going to need you to sign a release form. To get the tickets.

ZHAO: *(Tries to stand.)* Damn, man. What the hell'd you hit me with?

MAN: Did I say five-day pass? Let me make that a ten-day —

(KNOCK KNOCK KNOCK from the door.)

[YOLANDA: *(Offstage.)* Henry? Everything all right in there?]

HENRY: Dang it! Fine! It's all fine — we're . . . bonding!

[YOLANDA: I need to let the de-contam guys in —]

HENRY: Just a minute! We're at a very delicate stage!

ZHAO: What the hell's going on, man?

HENRY: *(Quietly.)* OK. To get the tickets, this is a very special trial offer, and to get the tickets, you need to not say anything to anyone out there. Not a sound. You understand? You can smile and nod. OK? Even if they . . . kind of strip you down and de-louse you.

ZHAO: What?

HENRY: Standard park procedure! Can't be too careful nowadays!

ZHAO: Look, I don't know the game here —

HENRY: No game! Just sign —

ZHAO: — but I know the smell of shit on shoes.

HENRY: What?

ZHAO: You stepped in something *bad,* man. I seen that expression on my friends before, usually right before their ass ends up in the pokey.

HENRY: I don't, I, I don't know what you're —

ZHAO: Look, man, I don't know what the hell you were doin' out there on the Rez with your Black Hawk whatever. But I know this. You want me to keep my mouth shut, it's gonna take a shitload more than a ten-day pass to fuckin' Culture Fiesta.

(Beat. They watch each other.)

HENRY: What do you want?

MAN: *(Points to the CD player.)* First, can the damn chanting and drumming. It's killin' me, man. Don't you got no "Bajos Bacas" or "Norteno Pimps"?

HENRY: *(Turns off the CD.)* No.

ZHAO: I gotta be honest with you — what's your name?

HENRY: Henry. Henry Carson.

ZHAO: Henrito. I was visiting my relatives 'cause I had a lot of free time and kind of needed to lay low.

HENRY: Yes.

ZHAO: I'm kind of between things right now.

HENRY: Yes . . .

ZHAO: I'm fuckin' unemployed, man. You want to keep my trap shut, you find me a job here with the Happy People.

HENRY: I don't — technically we're not hiring right now —

(BANG BANG BANG on the door.)

[YOLANDA: Henry, need I remind you of your increasingly perilous upcoming performance review?]

HENRY: One second! I think I just gained his trust!

(To Zhao.)

How would you feel about playing a Native American?

ZHAO: I am a Native American. Partly.

HENRY: If I can come up with the money, will you be WonderWorld's Native American?

ZHAO: Like in a stunt show with tomahawks and horses and shit?

HENRY: Like you sit around and get looked at and do Corn Grinding dances and chants and serve fry bread and mutton to tourists.

ZHAO: Like working at McDonald's.

HENRY: More singing and rug weaving, but yes.

ZHAO: What kind of salary?

HENRY: I don't know. We don't pay the other exhibits — just room and board — I have to take the money out of Native upkeep and maybe the Christmas party . . . maybe . . . ten dollars an hour?

ZHAO: You got yourself a deal, Henrito.

HENRY: Excellent!

ZHAO: But I don't speak hardly no Navajo.

HENRY: You can pick it up from discs and some of the other genuine natives.

ZHAO: The Navajo ones.

HENRY: Exactly. Don't hang around with the Central Kalapuyan or Tilamook. Just stay silent at first. You're a newbie, they'll expect some fear.

ZHAO: And I don't know shit about rugs or bowls.

HENRY: Turquoise?

(Zhao shakes his head.)

Don't you have *any* indigenous skills?

ZHAO: I rock at GameSplice and whiskey shots and *Brady Bunch* trivia.

HENRY: *(Winces.)* OK. We'll just — I'll get you books and DVDs. You can study them secretly in my office in off-hours.

ZHAO: Like a little espionage, huh?

HENRY: Oh God . . .

ZHAO: We used to play cowboys and Indians when we were pups in the irrigation ditches —

(Zhao moves like lightning, viciously "shooting" Henry, jamming his fingers into Henry's ribs and neck — Henry leaps back with a yell.)

ZHAO: *(Continued.)* Doov-Doov! Dooh-Dooh-Dooh-Dooh-Dooh-Dooh-

HENRY: Aaaaaa —

(It looks for a second like Zhao is about to go for a major artery . . .

then he pauses . . . grins a wicked grin and stands triumphantly over Henry who is sprawled over his desk.)

ZHAO: Somehow the Indians always ended up with AK-47s in our games.

HENRY: That's . . . that's great. Just . . . no shooting the tourists.

ZHAO: No way, man. I'm gonna be a good little Indian.

HENRY: Then . . . we have a deal?

ZHAO: The adventure begins today, my white brother.

(They shake hands.)

HENRY: Then let's go get you de-loused.

END OF SCENE

Natural Selection
Eric Coble

Comic

Henry, thirties to forties; Zhao, twenties to thirties

> *Henry is an executive at a vast theme park that, in a future time,*
> *seeks to preserve what's left of our cultural heritage. Henry has cap-*
> *tured Zhao, whom he thinks is a Native American, and brought*
> *him back to the park. But Zhao is not exactly what he had in mind.*

> *(Henry's office. Zhao walks in, still in traditional dress, but listening to*
> *an iPod. He flops down on a pillow.)*

HENRY: *(Holds up various papers.)* Can't you at least fill in the skill set forms?

ZHAO: Why?

HENRY: Because I'm already filling out your lineage, health, and psych forms!

ZHAO: So how crazy is this "Leonard Yazzie"?

HENRY: Zhao.

ZHAO: I'm cruisin' to this music, man. "The Bluebird Song," "Slow Round Dance." It speaks to me. In here.

> *(He pounds the rhythm on his chest.)*

HENRY: I'm glad.

ZHAO: You should be. You opened up a whole world to me.

HENRY: It's gonna shut back down if we don't get our ducks in a row.

ZHAO: *(Laughs.)* "Ducks in a row"

HENRY: Zhao!

ZHAO: I'll do it tomorrow.

HENRY: It's always tomorrow.

ZHAO: Must be a cultural thing, huh?

HENRY: Listen —

ZHAO: Chill down, Henrito. We're only gettin' a few people a day anyway.

HENRY: They'll come back. The rain will stop and they'll come back.

ZHAO: When's that gonna be? The old guys in the pavilion say it ain't stoppin'.

HENRY: Oh, where'd they get that — their extrasensory Native Doppler Radar?

ZHAO: Careful.

HENRY: Well, I mean, geez.

ZHAO: Those old guys know shit.

HENRY: Then why aren't you learning from them?

ZHAO: I am.

HENRY: Then weave a damn rug! Make a pot or a dream-catcher!

ZHAO: They're lookin' past that stuff now.

HENRY: What do you mean? They love doing crafts. They always smile and nod —

(Zhao laughs.)

HENRY: *(Continued.)* They were fine 'til you got here. Everything was fine 'til you got here.

ZHAO: I wasn't.

HENRY: Morale's going down the toilet. No one wants to work —

ZHAO: What can I say? They dig my style.

HENRY: The natives are getting surly.

ZHAO: Henry, Henry, Henry, man. Ya'ta' Hay, man. Breathe.

(Offering earphones.)

Listen to the music.

HENRY: I don't have time to listen to the music!

ZHAO: Then come with me. I'm on a hunt tonight.

HENRY: What?

ZHAO: I'm goin' foraging the Eastern Asian pavilions. I was cookin' with the Western Europe guys last night.

HENRY: What??

ZHAO: That German beer knocks your moccasins off, man. And the Spanish coffee! I could almost forgive 'em for what they did to Colorado and Mexico for that coffee —

HENRY: You can't. You can't visit other pavilions!

ZHAO: How come we got no rides, man? The Norwegians got this wooden boat trip past trolls and vikings and crap. How come the Native Americans got no ride?

HENRY: You've got a splendid movie —

ZHAO: We got no ride! You could do a little covered wagon train through history — past the Trail of Tears, the Long Walk, Wounded Knee. At the end you could sell little scalps and blankets infected with TB and whooping cough!

HENRY: See, this is why we find performers with limited English skills.

ZHAO: You wanta boost morale, put in a roller coaster or stunt show, man.

HENRY: How'd you get in the Norwegian pavilion?

ZHAO: I don't know. Someone gave me a pass.

HENRY: This doesn't happen. The tourists move from world to world. You stay put. Pure, untainted.

ZHAO: Henry, man, why you gotta make my job so hard?

HENRY: . . . Excuse me?

ZHAO: The egg's crackin', man, all you gotta do is get outta the way of the hammer.

HENRY: The only thing cracking is my patience with —

ZHAO: You invited me into your home, Henrito. We sloppy-joed together! Don't you dare damn that up —

HENRY: What's acceptable on my floor and what's acceptable in my office are two different things.

ZHAO: The Italian and French girls don't think so.

HENRY: No more. Give me back the pass.

ZHAO: I must've left it in my other loin cloth.

HENRY: I'm not kidding. If anyone caught you crossing borders —

ZHAO: They don't catch me. I'm on stealth, man. My paws are silent and my breath is clear.

HENRY: Give me the pass.

ZHAO: Or.

HENRY: You're my employee. Not Culture Fiesta's. Mine. They may eat this shit with mustard on the "Rez," but this is Henry Carson Land. You like the music, you like the old guys? You play by the rules. Or you'll be back on unemployment in Tucumcari.

(Pause. Zhao and Henry watch one another . . .)

ZHAO: Then I'll see you there. 'Cause once I go on TV about how a guy from WonderWorld shot me in the back while I was helping my old aunt and uncle, and he dragged me to work as a glorified robot Indian —

HENRY: You ungrateful sonofabitch — I selected you —

ZHAO: You want me to "get my ducks in a row"? You better fasten your fuckin' seat belt, asshole. You wanta keep filling out skill sheets and psych forms, keep fillin' — I just wanta be there when you see what water does to file cabinets and hard drives.

(He starts out.)

And I selected you, Henry. Not the other way round. I'll say hey to the Thai and Burmese girls for you.

END OF SCENE

The Tale of the Johnson Boys

Don Nigro

Dramatic
John and Henry, teens

> *John is the older brother, Henry the younger. Their families are poor settlers on the Ohio River in the 1790s. They've been captured by two Indians and taken away. Now it's night, by a campfire in the woods, and the Indians are sleeping, but John is awake and he has a plan to get away. He needs his sleepy brother Henry to cooperate, though.*

JOHN: Get up slow, Henry.

HENRY: What?

JOHN: Don't move fast, and don't make any noise. Slip out of his arms and get up slow.

HENRY: Why?

JOHN: Just do what I say and don't make any noise.

HENRY: OK. I was dreaming.

JOHN: It's time to go home now.

HENRY: They'll follow us and catch us again. They'll be mad at us then.

JOHN: They won't follow us.

HENRY: Yes they will, John, and they'll catch us, too, because they're Indians.

JOHN: They're not going to follow us because we're going to kill them before we go.

HENRY: We can't kill them. What if we kill one and the other one wakes up? He'll kill us then for sure.

JOHN: We'll kill both of them at the same time.

HENRY: How are we going to kill them both at the same time? There's only one gun. We can't kill them both at the same time. When you shoot the gun to kill the one, the other one will wake up.

JOHN: We'll kill one with the gun and the other with the tomahawk.

HENRY: We can't.

JOHN: Listen, Henry. We can't stand here and argue about it. They'll wake up. They're stronger than us. They're quicker than us. They know the woods better than us. The only advantage we got is right now, because they're so tired, they're sleeping and we're awake, and we're not too far from home yet. We might never catch them asleep again. They might meet up with more Indians tomorrow. We get much further away from home, we'll never find our way back. We got to kill them, Henry, and we got to do it right now.

HENRY: I don't want to.

JOHN: We got to.

HENRY: You do it.

JOHN: I can't do it by myself, Henry. Not both at the same time. You got to kill one of them.

HENRY: Can't you kill one with the tomahawk and then shoot the other one?

JOHN: The one I hit with the tomahawk might yell. If he yells and wakes up the other one we're dead. I thought it all through, Henry. You got to help me do this. And it's got to be right now.

END OF SCENE

Theatre District
Richard Kramer

Comic
Wesley and George, twenties to forties

George and Wesley are friends. Wesley wants to be more like George.

WESLEY: George? I'm not gay, you know.

GEORGE: I know.

WESLEY: Or I don't think so.

GEORGE: Well, things can change.

WESLEY: They can?

GEORGE: One day you're walking down Sixth Avenue and a *Big Gay Cloud*
    descends —

WESLEY: George — !

GEORGE: Sorry.

WESLEY: Nobody knows anything, George, do they?

GEORGE: It would seem that way.

WESLEY: Me, especially. Like, I never know who anyone is. But I
    know — I know who you are, George. And that whatever I become?
    Whoever I turn into?
        (A beat.)
        I want — to be like you.
    (A pause. George takes this in.)

GEORGE: Why would you want — that?

WESLEY: I don't mean like a big fag or anything! Not that you're that
    big —

GEORGE: Wesley? Listen to me. This is important. Fags come in one size.
    And it's always big.

WESLEY: George!

GEORGE: Sorry —

WESLEY: All I want to say is — I want to be how you are.

GEORGE: Which is — ?

WESLEY: I don't know! Just — *there*, I guess. Which you are. Which you've been. For me.

(He sees something. George sees him see it.)

GEORGE: What?

WESLEY: There! In that building. Someone's looking at us!

GEORGE: Oh! Him! I know him from the gym —

(Waves:)

Hi — !

WESLEY: *(Laughs.)* George!

GEORGE: What?

WESLEY: You're so embarrassing!

GEORGE: Thank you. So, I don't know about you, but it's gotten a little cold out here —

WESLEY: Yeah —

GEORGE: We should go in —

WESLEY: Hey, George — ?

GEORGE: *(Mock exhaustion.)* *More* questions?! What's left? Nature versus nurture? Influence of hypothalamus size —

WESLEY: *(Simply.)* Does my dad love me, George?

(A brief pause.)

GEORGE: Oh, yes.

WESLEY: Oh.

(A brief pause, then —)

WESLEY: You know, you're right. It is cold —

(He starts to exit.)

GEORGE: Wes? Wait.

(Wesley stops. He turns back to George.)

GEORGE: One more thing. You had one more question.

WESLEY: I did?

GEORGE: I never said — when you asked — about whether or not I think it's a choice.

(Gathers it together:)

Well — no.

WESLEY: No. So you mean like Dad said, because he said —

GEORGE: No. Not like him. Because — see — I don't even know what I want to say here — but when someone says "Of course it's not a choice, who would ever choose that —"

(A brief pause.)

I want to say — there's a lot of people, in this world, who would. There's *me. I* would. Because — Wesley?

(A beat.)

When you step into your life — through the door and you're *in* it, really *in* it, I just hope that you feel about your life the way I feel about mine. So you want to be like me? Be like me in that.

WESLEY: I'll try. I promise.

GEORGE: Good. 'Cause I'm freezing my ass off out here.

WESLEY: Yeah. Me, too . . . So I guess we should go in, huh?

GEORGE: I guess we should.

WESLEY: Yeah. We should.

(But they don't, not right away; they linger for a final moment. George moves to the edge of the roof, wrapping his arms around himself, his back turned to Wesley. A beat, then —)

WESLEY: Hey, George?

GEORGE: *(Without turning.)* Yeah?

WESLEY: I guess a lot can happen in a day, huh?

GEORGE: *(After a moment:)* Well — that's what days are for.

(Then, as they each become part of a Ninth Avenue night sky —)

END OF SCENE

Scenes for Two Women

Boar's Head

Don Nigro

Comic

Robin, twenties, dressed as a boy; Doll, could be any age

> *At the Boar's Head Inn, in Eastcheap, London, two characters from*
> *Shakespeare's* Henry IV *plays, Doll Tearsheet, the prostitute, and*
> *Robin, supposedly a serving boy, are waiting for Falstaff to come home*
> *from the wars. Doll doesn't know that Robin is actually a girl in*
> *disguise.*

ROBIN: Mistress Quickly is much distracted today, is she not, Doll?

DOLL: She is anxious to see Jack Falstaff back from the wars. Come here, boy, why don't you, and be closer to me.

ROBIN: *(Moving a step or two closer.)* Are you not hearing me well enough, Mistress Doll?

DOLL: No, boy, there is wax in my ears. Come closer.

ROBIN: *(Moving just a bit closer.)* The application of a reed and a bit of gentle scraping may work wonders for that, I have heard.

DOLL: *(Reaching out and yanking Robin closer.)* Come here, boy, and I will teach you a trick or two more pleasurable than removing ear wax.

ROBIN: *(Attempting to get away.)* Please, Doll. I am a good boy, and innocent of all womanish matters.

DOLL: Then you are greatly in need of the tutoring of one such as I, who has seen much, and done much —

ROBIN: I really must go, Mistress Doll.

DOLL: *(Yanking him down onto her lap.)* Not so fast, my shy little weasel. I like a shy boy. It is a sweet challenge to my powers of enlightenment. But before we properly begin your education, I must first examine your weapon.

(She reaches down between Robin's legs.)

ROBIN: YEOWWWW. Mistress, please.

DOLL: What's this? What mystery is this? Where is this? Have you so minis-
cule a worm I cannot locate it? If so, it would be the first time.

ROBIN: It's there, Miss. It is simply hiding from you.

DOLL: Trust me, boy, if I cannot find it, then it is not there. You poor
creature. What has happened to you? Was it a farming accident?

ROBIN: Umm, yes, Miss. The pig ate it. It was a hideous thing. I cannot
speak of it without weeping. Now, I really must go and —

DOLL: Wait a moment, wait a moment. What is this? And what are these?
I know what these are. These are not entirely unfamiliar to me. These
are breasts! This boy has got breasts! AHHH. IT IS A MOR-
PHODITE!

ROBIN: Be quiet, you silly girl. I see I am forced to tell you my secret, but
you must swear on pain of death to keep it.

DOLL: I love secrets, but I am made deeply uneasy by morphodites.

ROBIN: I am not a morphodite, and I am not a boy. I am a woman.

DOLL: A woman?

ROBIN: I was born one, and still am.

DOLL: Well, this explains why I had such uncommon difficulty in locat-
ing your pizzle.

ROBIN: You must keep this information to yourself, Doll. I beg you.

DOLL: I am confused. Then you lied about the pig?

ROBIN: I must confess, I did.

DOLL: But why put on this semi-mannish act?

ROBIN: I went to make my fortune at court, to see what a man's life might
be like, and serve the Prince, a person for whom I had much girlish
admiration, but the Prince gave me to Sir John Falstaff, who has sent
me in turn here to Mistress Quickly, while he is at the wars, in par-
tial payment for his drinking debts, and because he found me a great
distraction during battle. He said I lacked courage, but in truth it
was that he would always stumble over me and fall when he was running from the enemy.

DOLL: But why do you persist in this disguise?

ROBIN: I find I have grown more and more to relish the freedom of it.
As a man, I may go where I please and do what I please, at least after
the slops are emptied. As a girl, I could do nothing whatsoever but

be chaperoned here and worried over there and gaped at by imbeciles.

DOLL: But does not your family worry over you in your absence?

ROBIN: My father thinks me dead. I am thrown out upon fortune now, and you must keep my secret, or I am lost.

DOLL: Oh, dear. I think I was not made for keeping secrets. If God expected me to keep secrets, he should not have given me a mouth.

ROBIN: But you must, or the church will burn me as a witch, for wearing of men's clothing. So you must be silent, Doll. Will you, please?

DOLL: I shall do my best, as I should not wish to see you made into a pile of cinders by good Christian people, but I must warn you, boy, or whatever you may be, that keeping still is so much against my given nature, I fear that in the endeavor I shall do myself some serious internal injury.

END OF SCENE

Bourbon at the Border
Pearl Cleage

Dramatic
Rosa and May, thirties to forties

> *Rosa and May are neighbors. Rosa comes down and tries to get May to talk about her man, Charlie.*

ROSA: I thought you were going to call me.

MAY: Charlie just left a minute ago. I'm surprised you didn't see him in the hall.

ROSA: I wasn't sure if you had left a message and I never play them back when Ty stays over. All I need is for some old fool to resurface feeling frisky and leave me a message for old time's sake.

MAY: You ought to quit!

ROSA: So where is he?

MAY: He went out to look for work.

ROSA: *(Surprised.)* On Saturday morning?

MAY: He said they're hiring at Hudson's warehouse. Just until he can find something better.

ROSA: I saw that Hudson's notice in the paper yesterday, too. I started to go down there myself.

MAY: To the warehouse?

ROSA: Sonny's insurance ain't going as far as I hoped it would, rest in peace, and me and Tyrone drank up half my savings at the club last night. Now I know why he's always sneaking something in. Five dollars for bourbon and coke! And it's a crime what they're charging for a shot of cognac!

MAY: How was the show?

ROSA: Girl, don't get me started! We were so close when he started singing "Disco Lady," I could see the sweat pop out on his face. And guess what?

MAY: I'm scared to.

ROSA: When he sang "I Believe in You," he came over and picked up my hand and started singing it straight to me, I almost passed out.

MAY: That was probably all the expensive bourbon you were drinking.

ROSA: I swear that Negro is so fine if I'd been by myself he'd a had a helluva time getting rid of me. But enough about my night. What time did Brother Charles finally make his appearance?

MAY: Not long after you left.

ROSA: And?

MAY: And what?

ROSA: So how is he?

MAY: He's fine.

ROSA: That's it? He's fine?

MAY: That's it. He's fine. *(A beat.)*

ROSA: Do they think he'll try it again? *(A beat.)*

MAY: He won't try it again.

ROSA: How do you know?

MAY: *(Sharply.)* Because I won't let him. *(A beat.)* Want some coffee?

ROSA: Sure. *(A brief silence. Rosa cannot think of a way to get May to talk about Charlie, so she abandons the effort for the moment.)* You hear what happened?

MAY: What?

ROSA: They found a body downtown.

MAY: A body? Where?

ROSA: Right near the park.

MAY: No kidding? What happened?

ROSA: They don't know. No motive. No suspects.

MAY: Probably some more gang stuff.

ROSA: Not hardly. This was a white guy.

MAY: Really?

ROSA: An old white guy. Still had his wallet and his car keys on him.

MAY: What was he doing downtown?

ROSA: They still do business around here.

MAY: Not after this they won't.

ROSA: The cops are going to arrest everybody they even think might have done it.

MAY: All the men living in that park, they ought to have a field day.

ROSA: Tyrone said for me to be careful walking around by myself.

MAY: He's right.

ROSA: I'm always careful. I been running these streets all my life and I'm not going to quit now.

MAY: It's going to get worse before it gets better.

ROSA: You sound like that guy preaching in front of the grocery store, "There will be wars and rumors of wars."

MAY: I don't know about all that, but me and Charlie are not going to stick around for it, whatever it's going to be.

ROSA: Where are you going?

MAY: We're moving to Canada.

ROSA: To live?

MAY: Soon as I can talk Charlie into it.

ROSA: Have you ever been there?

MAY: It's right across the bridge. Haven't you?

ROSA: I went a couple of times, but what's the point, you know? Windsor ain't that much different from Detroit if you ask me.

MAY: It's different if you go out into the country.

ROSA: You moving to the woods?

MAY: Don't say it like that. It's beautiful.

ROSA: I can just see you and Charlie out there for about two weeks, then you'd come running back to the good old U.S.A.

MAY: Not a chance. Charlie's different over there. One time we rented a cabin. We woke up in the morning and there was so much snow we couldn't hardly see the car. The sun was out and the air was so clean you wanted to drink it like water. You'll have to come and visit us. Tyrone can come, too.

ROSA: Tyrone ain't hardly interested in no weekend in the woods.

MAY: You'd be surprised how different a man will act out in nature.

ROSA: Different how?

MAY: It brings out something good in them. Being in nature, knowing they're connected to something bigger.

ROSA: Bigger than what?

MAY: Say what you want, you'll be knocking on our door when the city gets too crazy to live in.

ROSA: It's already too crazy to live in, so what can you do?

MAY: You weren't really thinking about going down to the warehouse, were you?

ROSA: I surely was. Once I pay my rent and buy a couple bags of groceries, I'm all in.

MAY: They're hiring at the city.

ROSA: In the cafeteria?

MAY: No, night work.

ROSA: Night work doing what?

MAY: Cleanup or security.

ROSA: I am not hardly ready to start scrubbing floors and you know I ain't shooting nobody over something that don't even belong to me!

MAY: Suit yourself.

ROSA: If I tell you something, will you promise not to tell Tyrone?

MAY: What is it?

ROSA: You have to promise!

MAY: I promise.

ROSA: I interviewed for a phone sex job.

MAY: What?!

ROSA: Don't sound so shocked. You don't actually do anything. You just talk about it.

MAY: What did you say?

ROSA: Well, first they asked me if I had any hang-ups about anything. I said not as far as I know, then the guy started asking me —

MAY: A man interviewed you?

ROSA: He owns the place.

MAY: Go on . . .

ROSA: He asked me if I had ever faked an orgasm.

MAY: What'd you tell him?

ROSA: I told him no! *(May raises her eyebrows.)* Force of habit, OK? But I told him I was sure I could do it, so he started asking me about specific stuff and, girl, I swear, it was all I could do to keep from putting my fingers in my ears and running out the place.

MAY: Stuff like what?

ROSA: You know, animals and stuff.

MAY: Animals?

ROSA: It's a big world, honey. Everybody got a right to do their own thing.

MAY: Yeah, but animals?

ROSA: Don't worry. I told him I didn't know nothing about no animals and he said that was fine. They didn't get much call for that during the day anyway — I told him I could only work in the daytime — and how did I feel about S and M?

MAY: Did you tell him you were a Baptist?

ROSA: I told him I was a meat-and-potatoes kind of gal and if they specialized in all that freaky-deaky stuff I should probably take my business elsewhere.

MAY: Good for you!

ROSA: So he said everything was fine and asked me if I'd do an audition.

MAY: I thought you said it was just on the phone.

ROSA: It is, but you still got to audition. They aren't going to hook you up with a paying customer if you can't come through, no pun intended.

MAY: So what did you do?

ROSA: He put me in this little cubicle, like a telephone operator, you know, and then he called me up.

MAY: Jesus, Rose! Weren't you embarrassed?

ROSA: Nothing too weird, you know, he would tell me what he was gonna do to me and I had to moan and groan and act like it was driving me crazy to hear about it and then he started breathing real hard so I started breathing real had and that was about it.

MAY: I can just hear you huffin' and puffin'. "I think I can! I think I can!"

ROSA: I know I can! I even hollered a little at the end.

MAY: I can't believe you did this.

ROSA: You know guys like it when you scream. Makes them feel like they got you to give up something you been holding back.

MAY: Are you going to take the job?

ROSA: I told him I had to think about it. He told me I was a natural.

MAY: A natural what?

ROSA: Whatever! The weirdest part about it was — don't laugh! — I really got into it.

MAY: I don't want to hear this.

ROSA: It was like dancing or something. All I had to do was follow his lead.

MAY: I think you can do better.

ROSA: Yeah, how? Sweeping up at City Hall after you unionized day workers have gone home?

MAY: Cleanup isn't so bad. At least it's quiet and you get to work by yourself.

ROSA: I don't see you running down to apply for the job.

MAY: I already did.

ROSA: Did what?

MAY: Applied for night crew. I been working three nights a week all summer. With Charlie being away, I needed something to do and we can use the money.

ROSA: I ain't never loved no man enough to work two jobs for him.

MAY: It won't be long. Soon as Charlie gets something, I'll quit.

ROSA: You want me to ask this guy at the sex shop if he's got another opening?

MAY: No, thanks. I couldn't do that.

ROSA: You too high-class to fake it?

MAY: It's not that. I just think some things are private.

ROSA: You're a romantic, May. You know that? All for love!

MAY: That's not a bad thing, is it?

ROSA: No. It's kind of sweet actually. Impractical, but kind of sweet. I don't think I ever felt that way.

MAY: Not even about Sonny?

ROSA: Maybe at the beginning, but not enough to be scrubbin' no floors to prove it.

MAY: *(Defensive.)* I'm not proving anything.

ROSA: Then what are you — May! I've got a proposition for you.

MAY: I'm fine, really.

ROSA: Charlie's looking for a job, right?

MAY: Right.

ROSA: And the doctor says it's OK, right?

MAY: Right.

ROSA: Well, last night, Ty was talking about how his boss was looking for a couple of new drivers and did he know anybody.

MAY: Are you serious?

ROSA: Serious as a heart attack. This guy and Ty were in the war together and to hear him tell it, they thick as thieves. Ty thinks the guy might even take him on as a partner pretty soon.

MAY: He wouldn't have to be out on the road a lot, would he?

ROSA: *(Amused.)* You really got it bad, girl, you know that? Don't worry, he'd be right here in town. They always start the new guys off local.

MAY: Do you think Tyrone would really put in a good word for him?

ROSA: If I asked him to, but there's something I gotta ask you first and you gotta tell me the truth.

MAY: What is it?

ROSA: Is he really OK?

MAY: Rose, you know I got no reason to lie to you. This morning when we were talking, he seemed like his old self again. He was really Charlie.

ROSA: But how can they be sure?

MAY: I'm sure.

ROSA: Oh, you're sure. The man is home one night and you're sure. *(A beat.)*

MAY: I'm not trying to talk you into anything. You brought it up to me, remember?

ROSA: You're right, you're right! OK, honey, here's what we'll do. Ty's coming by after work. Did you two kill that bourbon he left here yesterday?

MAY: We didn't touch it.

ROSA: Good. I'll bring him down to meet Charlie, we'll drink up that bourbon with you and see how they get along, then Ty can decide.

MAY: Should I tell Charlie?

ROSA: Of course. Make sure he's on his best behavior.

MAY: How much does Ty know?

ROSA: Not much. I told him Charlie had a bum leg they had to put a pin in. Rehab took longer than they expected it to.

MAY: Nothing else?

ROSA: I figure everybody got a right to tell their own business without no help from me. Besides, Charlie never tries anything on the job, does he?

MAY: No. He always comes home.

ROSA: So! No problem.

MAY: Thanks. Rosa.

ROSA: Don't thank me 'til he gets the job. What time is it?

MAY: Almost eleven.

ROSA: Already? I got a hair appointment at eleven-thirty and if I miss this girl, she won't wait for me. I'll see you later!

MAY: Around three?

ROSA: Make it four. I'll make sure he's in a good mood when we get down here.

MAY: Why don't you just call him?

ROSA: Go to hell!

(Rosa exits as lights go to black.)

END OF SCENE

Bulrusher
Eisa Davis

Dramatic
Bulrusher and Vera, late teens; both black

> *Bulrusher, a light-skinned black orphan, has done without love most*
> *of her life — until she meets Vera, the niece of a neighbor.*

BULRUSHER: She is a mirror.

VERA: *(Singing under Bulrusher's words.)* For all we know

BULRUSHER: A mirror. Schoolch never allowed any mirrors in the house.

VERA: This may only be a dream.

BULRUSHER: I always think about touching her skin. It's just like mine only smoother.

VERA: We come and we go, like the ripples on a stream

BULRUSHER: She says that I am beautiful. She says she wants to stretch herself over me like taffy so everyone can see my sweetness. But I want to do that to her.

VERA: So love me tonight, tomorrow was made for some

BULRUSHER: I don't care about anything else.

VERA: Tomorrow may never come, for all we know

BULRUSHER: We sell fruit.

VERA: *(Speaking to unseen customer.)* They're sweet. Nickel a piece.
    (As the scene continues, they do not speak to each other, but they continue to be in their own separate worlds.)

BULRUSHER: I eat with her every day, pick her up from her uncle's house by Barney Flats.

VERA: I have never been served food by a white woman before. I sat at the table with my napkin folded in my lap and she poured milk into my glass.

BULRUSHER: I take her with me to Cloverdale and we buy oranges and lemons and bananas and she sings next to me in the truck. Once she put her fingers on my knee and spelled my name up my thigh.

VERA: Bulrusher, why don't we go to the beach? Can't you see us running along the sand and tearing off our stockings?

BULRUSHER: One day she kissed my cheek to say good-bye. I grabbed her hand.

VERA: I'm saving up my money. And I eat anything I want. Sometimes just bread with mustard.

BULRUSHER: She wants to go to the ocean with me but I don't like the ocean. That's where my mother wanted me to die. You're my river. I'll bring Vera to you instead.

(The river. Bulrusher and Vera now talk to each other.)

BULRUSHER: *(To Vera.)* I guess I can tell everybody else's future because I don't know my own past. I was supposed to die, but I didn't, so I think I got an open ticket to the land of could be.

VERA: You like reading water?

BULRUSHER: Only if the person want to know the future. If she don't then it's all garbled up, can't read a thing. Image gets blurry, blinds me even. *(She picks up a twig and turns it on Vera.)* Sometimes I wish I did water witching instead 'cause no one ever minds finding water and water never minds being found.

(They laugh.)

Have you ever tried wild blackberries? Here.

VERA: They're sour.

BULRUSHER: They're almost ready.

VERA: What about these?

BULRUSHER: Poison.

VERA: And these? They smell like being sick.

BULRUSHER: Just juniper berries. If you're sick, you need these eucalyptus leaves. They'll cure anything that's hurtin' your chest from inside.

VERA: This water'll cure me!

(Vera takes off her clothes and jumps into the river in her slip.)

VERA: I just want to be clean. I'm clean here, right? You can see I'm clean.

BULRUSHER: Yeah, I can see.

VERA: then why aren't you getting in?

BULRUSHER: I don't know.

VERA: There're fish!

BULRUSHER: Stand in the sand.

VERA: It's deep.

BULRUSHER: There's a branch above you, hold onto that.

VERA: Nobody else come down here?

BULRUSHER: Only me. This is my secret place on the river.

VERA: Your river. It's your diary, your church, your everything.

BULRUSHER: Yeah, has been.

VERA: Well, your river is making me cold, so you should get in.

BULRUSHER: It's not cold, you're in the sun.

VERA: I don't want to die in here.

BULRUSHER: Why would you die?

VERA: Because it's quiet. Everything's so quiet. It makes me want to cry.
(Vera laughs.)

BULRUSHER: The river holds you. Anything that you are scared of, it'll hold
for you. I asked the river to save me when I was a baby girl, and it
held me.

VERA: Is that why you won't get in? You're scared your luck will run out?

BULRUSHER: I've just never taken anyone down to this water. I always come
here alone to talk and listen and I don't know how to do that with
you here too.
(Vera starts to get out.)

BULRUSHER: No, you stay, I just can't get in with you.

VERA: I'm done. I got in and I'm gettin' out.

BULRUSHER: Stay in longer, it's only been a minute.

VERA: Nothing to do if you're not in with me. Can't splash, can't play —
and I don't hear the river saying things like you do so I suppose I'm
just a little less entertained.

BULRUSHER: Wait — don't get out. I'll put my feet in.

VERA: I'm naked as a plucked chicken in an apron! You take off your
clothes too.

BULRUSHER: Why?

VERA: Because we're here together. So we're gonna do the same thing.
*(Bulrusher takes off her shoes. She takes off her shirt and then Vera pulls
off her trousers for her. Bulrusher is startled then begins to laugh. She
dives in wearing her undershirt and bloomers.)*

VERA: You don't wear a bra?

BULRUSHER: What's that?

VERA: For to keep your chest up. They'll start draggin' in the dust if you don't strap those things.

BULRUSHER: I didn't know you were supposed wear anything else.

VERA: You have been raised by wolves and none of 'em female.

(Bulrusher touches one of Vera's scars.)

BULRUSHER: What are these scars?

VERA: From my mama tryin' ta straighten my hair with a hot comb. But I'm a country girl now. Can get my hair wet as I want. Handstand! *(When Vera comes up, Bulrusher touches Vera's neck. Vera holds Bulrusher's hand to her wet neck and collarbone.)*

VERA: Have you ever noticed that white people smell like mayonnaise?

BULRUSHER: You don't want to go back to Birmingham.

VERA: Some days I could kill them all.

BULRUSHER: You're scared.

VERA: White folks are the ones should be scared 'cause we ain't takin' what they're servin' much longer. If they'd just read the Bible sometime they'd see what's coming for 'em.

BULRUSHER: Your mother misses you; she will cut her finger on the edge of a letter. But it isn't from you, it's a notice from a contest at the radio station.

VERA: I entered it in May.

BULRUSHER: You'll win a year supply of Dixie Peach Pomade and a subscription to *Jet* magazine. What's all that?

(Vera takes Bulrusher's hand off of her neck.)

BULRUSHER: I'm sorry.

VERA: You didn't ask if you could do that.

BULRUSHER: I didn't mean to.

VERA: That wasn't fair. I can't see *your* future.

BULRUSHER: It just happened. I couldn't read if you didn't want me to. I just wanted to touch your skin — like you wanted me to.

VERA: So what? So my mother didn't send me here. So I came here on my own. But that isn't all you saw.

BULRUSHER: No.

VERA: Then say it. Say what I already know.

BULRUSHER: It doesn't matter.

VERA: I wanna hear you say it.

BULRUSHER: I said I'd take care of you, that ain't gonna change now.

VERA: Say it.

BULRUSHER: I'll start tellin' fortunes again, make us some money — you don't have to worry 'bout nothin'.

VERA: You can't fix everything! Some things are just wrong and always will be.

BULRUSHER: Not you.

VERA: Yeah me.

BULRUSHER: So that's why you're here.

VERA: Don't make me explain. Just say it. Say it.

BULRUSHER: You're gonna have a baby. A boy.

VERA: A boy?

BULRUSHER: But I won't let you stand up to work, I'll do all the lifting. You can just sit and count the money.

VERA: I'm not gonna have a boy. Or a girl.

BULRUSHER: Yes you are. And he's gonna be as pretty as you.

VERA: I don't want it. All I need is the money to get rid of it.

BULRUSHER: He's yours. Don't say that.

VERA: Then you don't really want to help me.

BULRUSHER: Why would you want to get rid of a child?

VERA: You don't know where it came from.

BULRUSHER: But he's in you now.

VERA: I don't care 'cause I'll never love it.

BULRUSHER: You can just give him to me.

VERA: No! I never want to see its face! If you don't want to help me, that's fine. That's fine.

(Vera gets out of the water. Bulrusher follows her, quiet.)

VERA: If you tell anybody —

BULRUSHER: I won't.

(Bulrusher turns away from Vera. They both put on their clothes in silence.)

VERA: Bulrusher.

(Bulrusher turns toward her and Vera buttons Bulrusher's shirt. Vera kisses her.)

VERA: I guess I can't hide anything from you, huh.

(She kisses Bulrusher again. Bulrusher falls against Vera, crying. Vera kisses Bulrusher's tears.)

Bulrusher
Eisa Davis

Dramatic
Bulrusher, late teens; Madame, late thirties to early forties

> *When she was a baby, Bulrusher was put into a basket by her mother*
> *and floated down the river. She has never known who her mother*
> *is — until now.*

(Madame appears in a blue hat.)

MADAME: We don't look nothing alike.

(Bulrusher spins around to her.)

BULRUSHER: Blue hat.

MADAME: Is that gun for me?

BULRUSHER: Madame.

MADAME: Yeah. Don't call me anything different.

BULRUSHER: Madame.

MADAME: A gun. Where'd you get all these violent impulses?

BULRUSHER: Ma-dame.

MADAME: Yeah. *(Pause.)* Well don't stand there dumb, let's us have a conversation. Ain't you saved up some questions for me?

(Pause.)

BULRUSHER: No.

MADAME: I know you got some curiosity.

(Pause.)

BULRUSHER: When you leaving?

MADAME: You know I say that every summer when the heat gets to me.
Gave Schoolch his money back. I can't leave none a you. So you glad
it's me? Coulda been someone you couldn't relate to, somebody lack-
ing morals and accountability.

BULRUSHER: I just — what you —

MADAME: Spit it out.

BULRUSHER: How could — I don't – this ocean air is trying to kill me —

MADAME: No it ain't. You can talk.

BULRUSHER: I don't got any questions. I got to go.

MADAME: Bulrush, hold on. We don't gotta change nothing, let's just talk a while.

BULRUSHER: I got to go. Vera.

MADAME: I still have that basket I wove you. Went down and picked it up after Lucas found you. Wove it from reeds and rushes I found near Clear Lake when my ma was sick. You kept growin' in me, she passed, then you were born. Thought it would be nice for you to float in that basket and look up at the sky. But I was greedy. I had to spend a few days with you before I sent you off; had to see what of Lucas made it into you.

BULRUSHER: Vera and I are cousins?

MADAME: Kiss kiss,

BULRUSHER: I've got to tell her.

MADAME: Bulrush —

BULRUSHER: I'm going!

(Madame grabs Bulrusher by the shoulders.)

MADAME: Lucas took Vera to the train. She's going back to Birmingham.

BULRUSHER: I can catch her.

MADAME: No you can't.

BULRUSHER: Why not?

MADAME: The train left yesterday.

BULRUSHER: What about the baby.

MADAME: What about it. It's up to her.

(Bulrusher pulls all the money out of her pockets and throws it into the ocean.)

MADAME: Now what did you do that for?

BULRUSHER: You sent me down the river like I wasn't nothing but shorn hair. White whore didn't want her colored baby.

MADAME: I ain't white, my ma's a Pomo Indian. The rest I hope you'll let me make up for.

BULRUSHER: I always wished you were my ma. But why should I want you now?

MADAME: You don't have to.

BULRUSHER: I got plenty of shame. Plenty. And now you want to scrape some more off your shoe and rub it on me. You ain't nothing. Nothing but shame.

MADAME: That's right. Think my mother wanted me to be a businesswoman? Think I could have kept my business with folks knowing I was an Indian? I made my choice, stuck to it by her deathbed. Wasn't going to put you through all that I knew. Wasn't going to have no customer's baby. And I wasn't tryin' to lose no customer named Lucas.

BULRUSHER: You made Vera go away.

MADAME: No.

BULRUSHER: You told Lucas the truth, that I'm his?

MADAME: No, I told him I would marry him.

BULRUSHER: He wouldn't marry you if he knew about me.

MADAME: I guess I wanted to clear it with you — see if you want another father.

BULRUSHER: I ain't givin' up Schoolch.

MADAME: You don't have to.

BULRUSHER: You already turned Schoolch down. He should have somebody in' this world.

MADAME: He has what he's always had. I wish I wanted Schoolch, 'cause he never wanted to be a customer. And he never used you against me. Raised you with pure intent, followed you like a calling.

BULRUSHER: You didn't follow *me* down the river, I did that by myself.

MADAME: What do you want me to say?

BULRUSHER: I want you to apologize for trying to kill me.

MADAME: I didn't want you dead.

BULRUSHER: Then why did you get rid of me like that? I was floating for an eternity.

MADAME: You can't remember that.

BULRUSHER: Yes I can. Yes I can. I remember floating in' the night, the fog and the coyotes — didn't know what that sound was then but now I do. Mr. Jeans found me at Barney Flats, but I was there for days. I begged to be found. I talked to the sun with my fingers, kept closing my fist around it every time it went down trying to keep it with me. But the night would always come. And the river was so thin there, deep as a teardrop — but I kept myself alive. Why? To find you? To lose the only one who ever really touched me? Schoolch never did. He's a teacher, he doesn't know how. Only told me to sit up straight. Vera touched me, gave me softness and you made her leave. You knew she was going when I saw her last, didn't you. *(Madame is silent.)* Of course you did. So is she gonna kill her baby or be the preacher's wife who got raped by a cop?

MADAME: You're angry with me.

BULRUSHER: I'm not angry. I'm gonna kill you. I want to kill something. Walk toward the edge of that bluff. Do it.

(Madame doesn't move and Bulrusher aims her shotgun.)

BULRUSHER: Back to me. Go to the ocean and look at it.

(Madame walks to the edge of the cliff.)

BULRUSHER: See it gnashing its teeth? It wants you. Didn't want me. But it still wants to eat. Salt gonna sting your eyes, gonna burn you. All that seaweed down there is gonna grab you and drown you.

MADAME: Bulrusher.

BULRUSHER: You already dead, ever since you tried to kill me. You been dead.

MADAME: Bulrush —

BULRUSHER: Dead for money. Wanted some damn money steada me. Well go get it. I threw it in there for you. It's all yours.

MADAME: Bulrusher, I named you.

BULRUSHER: Bulrusher, caught in the bulrushes, abandoned to the weeds. I'm a weed.

MADAME: You got a name. You ain't a weed.

BULRUSHER: Jeans? Whore? Sneeble? Witch?

MADAME: You got my mama's name. You got your grandma's name just like she wanted you to have it.

BULRUSHER: Pomo? Indian? I don't want it.

MADAME: You got her name. It's Xa-wena. Means on the water.

BULRUSHER: You called me that once. One day.

MADAME: You remember.

BULRUSHER: I remember everything.

MADAME: *(Chants softly.)* O beda-Xa, a thi shishkith, ometh ele'le'. Xa-wena ewe-ba ke katsilith'ba ele'ledith. O beda-Xa, a thi boshtotsith.
(Speaks.) River water, I ask you, protect her, help her. Take her

to your bosom. Save her from the night and cold, river water, protect her. I thank you.

(Madame turns around. Bulrusher has lowered her shotgun.)

I prayed for you in your basket. And your river listened. She listened. The river's your mother. I throw stones into it every day to thank her for caring for you.

(Madame kneels and hugs Bulrusher's legs.)

MADAME: See? I got softness.

(Pause.)

BULRUSHER: Xa-wena.

MADAME: Yes?

BULRUSHER: I was just sayin' it.

MADAME: Oh.

END OF SCENE

Frame 312
Keith Reddin

Dramatic
Lynette, twenties; Doris, twenties to thirties

> *This scene takes place on a train, shortly after the Kennedy assassination. Lynette is a photo lab technician, who has seen the missing frame 312 of the Zapruder film of the assassination. She is scared to death.*

(Lynette on the train to New York. Next to her sits Doris.)

DORIS: They came to the front door.

LYNETTE: When?

DORIS: In the night. You hear the doorbell ring, the first thing you think . . .

LYNETTE: Something bad has happened.

DORIS: They were standing there and I turn on the porch light and Phil — that's my husband — he's standing next to me . . .

LYNETTE: Were they in uniform?

DORIS: Who?

LYNETTE: The police.

DORIS: No, they were in . . . suits. Dark suits.

LYNETTE: They were detectives.

DORIS: I asked for some sort of identification.

LYNETTE: To make sure.

DORIS: They could be . . .

LYNETTE: Anyone. And what did they say? . . .

DORIS: They said we have some terrible news.

LYNETTE: Oh.

DORIS: And I said, is this about . . . is it about Michael?

LYNETTE: You knew.

DORIS: I thought these people here, in the dead of night . . .

LYNETTE: Yes.

DORIS: Somebody shot him. They shot my brother in some bar. He's in the hospital.

LYNETTE: But he's alive.

DORIS: Nothing makes sense. People shooting each other.

LYNETTE: Even the president.

DORIS: I went to the Capitol. I waited in line to pay my respects.

LYNETTE: It won't stop there.

DORIS: What do you mean?

LYNETTE: The president, that's only the beginning.

DORIS: The beginning of what?

LYNETTE: Of something terrible. *(Beat.)* I shouldn't have told you.

DORIS: I just want to see my brother.

LYNETTE: He's alive. Just remember that.

DORIS: You're right.

LYNETTE: Other people might not live.

DORIS: What are you saying?

LYNETTE: Do you know why I went to Washington, D.C. today?

DORIS: I don't.

LYNETTE: I'm going to tell you something. My name is Lynette. Lynette Porter. I want you to remember my name.

DORIS: I . . .

LYNETTE: Say my name.

DORIS: Lynette Porter.

LYNETTE: Remember what I look like.

DORIS: I should . . . we're almost at the station.

LYNETTE: If one day you read in the paper that I died. If they say my car crashed, or I burned in a fire. Remember.

DORIS: There are people meeting me.

LYNETTE: Whatever you read. It's not the truth.

DORIS: Why do you say that?

LYNETTE: Because I know things.

DORIS: You're not making sense.

LYNETTE: They can kill presidents.

DORIS: Who?

LYNETTE: They won't stop there.

DORIS: Please . . .

LYNETTE: What hospital is your brother in?

DORIS: I don't understand . . .

LYNETTE: Tell me the hospital.

DORIS: Lenox Hill.

LYNETTE: And where is it located? The hospital?

DORIS: East 75th?

LYNETTE: Lenox Hill Hospital is located on East 77th Street.

DORIS: I meant 77th. I was confused . . . (. . .)

LYNETTE: Just read the paper. If you see my picture, you'll know.

DORIS: I'm sorry if I . . . I just needed someone to talk to.

LYNETTE: Your brother will recover.

DORIS: I pray he will.

LYNETTE: Just remember what we talked about. It's important to remember.

DORIS: I will.

LYNETTE: That's all we can do.

END OF SCENE

Indoor/Outdoor
Kenny Finkle

Comic
Matilda, thirties to forties; Samantha, twenties, a cat

> *Matilda works in a vet's office but fancies herself something of a ther-*
> *apist. She is able to talk to, and understand, cats — which is for-*
> *tunate because Samantha is a cat. Matilda is trying to find out why*
> *Samantha is so unhappy with her owner, Shuman.*

MATILDA: OK. Samantha, private conference with me over here.
   (Samantha follows Matilda to another side of the room.)
MATILDA: Now, Samantha, where were we?
SAMANTHA: We were talking about Oscar.
MATILDA: Oscar. Right. Who's Oscar?
SAMANTHA: An alley cat. We're in love.
MATILDA: Oh my.
SAMANTHA: As soon as I get out of here, we're going away together. You
   ruined everything when you showed up. Shuman was just about to
   throw me out.
MATILDA: Oh my.
SAMANTHA: I'm not happy here Matilda. I don't want to make this work.
   I'm not meant to be an indoor cat. I'm an outdoor cat.
MATILDA: But how do you know?
SAMANTHA: I killed a mouse. I — I'm a wild tigress. I'm —
MATILDA: Oh my.
SAMANTHA: So you have to help me Matilda. You have to help me get
   out of here. Distract Shuman or something. Open the door for me.
   Let me be free to be with the cat I love! To be my true self. To love!
   To live!
MATILDA: But what about Shuman?
SAMANTHA: I've been trying to get away from him ever since I got back

from meeting you. He's bad for me. He doesn't care for me. He doesn't know me. I need to be known. I need to be —

MATILDA: Oh my.

SAMANTHA: So will you help me get out of here?

(Beat.)

MATILDA: No. No Samantha I won't help you leave.

SAMANTHA: You won't?

MATILDA: No, I'm going to help you stay.

SAMANTHA: Why?

MATILDA: Because there's something worth fighting for here.

SAMANTHA: How can you say that? You have no idea what Oscar makes me feel, you have no idea how I've felt here. I feel compromised, I feel like — like I've settled. I don't want to settle Matilda.

MATILDA: How is staying and letting yourself be known to Shuman settling?

SAMANTHA: I feel like you don't understand me.

MATILDA: I feel like maybe you don't understand yourself.

(Quite suddenly, Samantha bites Matilda . . . Hard.)

MATILDA: OW!!!! Oh! You little . . . Samantha! Oh!!!!! . . .

MATILDA: She bit me! Samantha bit me! . . .

MATILDA: Bad girl! No. Not bad girl. That's bad to say. You're not a bad girl. You're just confused. You're lost. You're — I'm — I'm – I must, I must breathe. Breathe Matilda. *(She does some of the Lamaze breathing.)* Let's just get this all out in the open. Shuman, Samantha is in love with an alley cat named Oscar.

END OF SCENE

Kerry and Angie
Gerry Sheridan

Seriocomic
Kerry and Angie, late thirties to early forties

> *Two long-time friends attend a christening together. While barely
> following the service, Kerry confronts Angie about her sexual behavior
> since the death of her husband.*

> *(The stage is set with two rows of chairs on a slight diagonal to indi-
> cate pews in a church. Scene opens with Kerry and Angie entering. They
> are carrying programs that say "Holy Mary Church" with a big black
> cross on the front. They are dressed up. Angie might not be dressed en-
> tirely appropriately for a christening. At some point during the play she
> might remove her jacket and be wearing a very revealing top. Angie has
> a Duane Reade bag and a Starbucks bag from which she surreptitiously
> drinks a cup of coffee during the service. Enter Kerry and Angie, talk-
> ing while they enter from backstage to partial light.)*

KERRY: I can't believe you're so late, I've been waiting outside for twenty
minutes.

ANGIE: It couldn't be helped. I had a hard day.

KERRY: Where, at Duane Reade? You're late all the time.

ANGIE: Maybe I'm busier than most people.

KERRY: WHAT!

> *(Lights come up on them when suddenly they realize they are in a church
> and everyone is looking at them.)*

KERRY: Where do you want to sit?

ANGIE: Let's sit back here.

KERRY: We can't sit back here.

ANGIE: Why not?

KERRY: It's too far back.

ANGIE: So what?

KERRY: Look, they're gesturing for us to come down front.

ANGIE: I can't sit down front. If I have to stare at a baby for an hour with everyone with tears in their eyes I'm gonna fucking kill myself. Look, make the humble gesture. *(She waves off people down front.)* I'll cough to seal the deal — no one wants germs around a baby. CAAAAAAAA CAAAAA CAAA!!!!! Sit!

(Angie sits in very last row (stage right chair) — Kerry kneels and crosses herself and sits in the row in front of Angie (stage left chair) and places her baby gift bag on the seat next to her.)

ANGIE: It's all so tribal. This christening business. Do they really think it makes any difference if if they pour water over the poor sucker's head?

KERRY: I try not to think about it.

ANGIE: You haven't called me this week what have you been doing?

(Angie takes out a cup of Starbucks and drinks from it while hiding behind a program.)

KERRY: Nothing.

ANGIE: Oh.

KERRY: Really, nothing. The only thing I accomplished today was I trimmed my dog's toe hairs.

ANGIE: Hah.

KERRY: I did go to the gym but then I got tired and I had to take a nap. Then I had lunch delivered 'cause I was too tired to cook. Oh, oh! And I read the *Post* for the first time today and I learned that there is a dog in my neighborhood on Prozac and that a woman in Argentina got a fifty-year-old fetus removed.

ANGIE: Get out.

KERRY: I swear. And now I think I should start reading it all the time 'cause who knows what kind of important facts I'm missing every day. I'm a little down I guess. On top of that I got a horrible haircut. It's like a mullet or something.

ANGIE: It's not that bad.

KERRY: Yeah it is. So my big purpose in life right now is growing out my last hairdo. I'm sorry, I should be trying to cheer you up.

ANGIE: That's all right. When this is over I'm gonna have a stiff drink.

(They both cross themselves while following the service.)

ANGIE: There was an article in *Vogue* that I saw the other day — the title of it was "Confidence, Power, Sex Appeal All in One Bottle." I was like oh — someone's finally writing a realistic article about booze, and it was about perfume — isn't that funny?

KERRY: I'm sorry I didn't hear a word you said. Do I look like Franken- stein? I can't stop thinking about my hair.

(Angie's cell phone rings. Angie digs through her bag searching for the phone. She finds it and answers it.)

ANGIE: Hello? Oh hi? How are you? Miss me already? I'm at a christen- ing with a friend — you wanna join us after it's over? Huh? Oh. No, I didn't notice. I was rushing around getting ready to go out. Oh, OK. Yeah, I'll leave it with the doorman. No problem. Bye. *(Angie hangs up the phone and throws it in her purse.)* Fuck Fuck Fuck Fucker.

KERRY: What's wrong?

ANGIE: Nothing. Forget it.

KERRY: Angie.

ANGIE: What?

KERRY: That was some guy you brought home last night wasn't it?

ANGIE: Look, it's no big deal.

KERRY: Yes it is. You promised me no more one-night stands.

ANGIE: OK OK.

KERRY: No — you promised. I don't believe it. You cried. I cried. You swore. I can't believe it. I'm not kidding Angie. This is creepy.

(Angie gets up and goes to sit in Kerry's row, ducking while walking so people don't see her.)

ANGIE: Oh please. What's the difference? I don't think it makes any dif- ference what we do. You know what life is? You eat, sleep and die. So who cares? Since Frankie died I feel like nothing means anything.

KERRY: Well it does.

ANGIE: Yeah? Well, what does it mean?

KERRY: Um, ah . . . OK, look, forget about meaning — I just can't be- lieve you're happy bringing home strange guys all the time. This can't make you feel good about yourself.

ANGIE: No, but it feels good at the moment.

KERRY: What, you can't go without sex?

ANGIE: Sex? Sex has nothing to do with it. Sex is just an excuse for being held for a few hours.

KERRY: Oh.

ANGIE: Look, you don't know what it's like to lose a husband.

(Angie gets up and goes back to her seat.)

KERRY: I'm single, believe me I know what it's like to be alone.

ANGIE: It's not the same. The alone of widowhood is much worse than the alone of single. You have nothing to compare it to. I've thought about it, OK? I even went to church on Sunday to pray about it after bringing home some guy at four A.M. who was outta there by six. My doorman must get an eyeful believe you me. Anyway, I prayed about it and I think God understands I'm not ready to stop yet.

KERRY: Oh, uh huh. Well, we're all worried about you Angie.

ANGIE: All? Who all?

(They both stand — part of the service.)

KERRY: Well, Maryann even talked to me about it.

ANGIE: Maryann? Hah — she's no angel either, believe you me.

KERRY: That's not the point.

ANGIE: Oh really? Well it sounds like she's talking about me.

(Angie starts to walk down the aisle toward Maryann — Kerry stops her.)

ANGIE: Who is she to talk?

KERRY: What? We're not talking about Maryann.

ANGIE: Yea, well I could tell you a few things about her, one of them involving a stranger and some self-tanning lotion.

KERRY: Would you stop!

(Kerry makes Angie sit down with her.)

KERRY: Don't take your own guilt out on Maryann.

ANGIE: I'm not guilty. She's the one who should be guilty. The guy was engaged and she brought him to my apartment 'cause of her kids and they used my self tanning lotion as lubricant 'cause he wanted to do anal or something — I found it on the bed when I got home. Ueww. I told her I hope he didn't end up going home with an orange dick 'cause how was he gonna explain that to his girlfriend?

KERRY: I so didn't need to know this.

ANGIE: Yes, you do. Because she's talking about me like I'm the only one and I'm sorry but one butt fuck with a stranger is equal to about fifty one-night stands.

KERRY: OK OK — forget Maryann.

ANGIE: And she's been divorced three times — at least Frankie stayed with me the whole time while he was still alive.

KERRY: Oh God, Angie. *(Moves closer.)* I still can't believe Frankie's dead.

ANGIE: I know.

KERRY: I loved him too Angie. He was the best.

ANGIE: I know.

KERRY: No one can handle you the way Frankie handled you.

ANGIE: He was a prince.

KERRY: You guys were perfect together.

ANGIE: He didn't care that I couldn't cook.

KERRY: Yea, he thought it was funny.

ANGIE: Sometimes I'm so pissed off that he died.

KERRY: Of course you are. I kept thinking he was gonna get better.

ANGIE: That's the only thing I feel bad about with all these guys, like maybe Frankie's watching me. Although if he is, I wish he'd send a nice guy my way.

KERRY: You have to make room in your life for the nice guy. It doesn't help having a life of one-night stands and dating twenty-two-year-olds.

ANGIE: I can't help it if dim lighting in bars makes twenty-two-year-olds approach me.

KERRY: Yes, you can. Look, think about this, I read about this experiment where they couldn't train blue jays not to keep gobbling up a tiny chunk of food instead of waiting a short time for a much bigger piece. They did like a thousand repetitions. Can you just see it? Peck, crumb, peck crumb, peck crumb, like a thousand times? That's what you're doing. Crumb, crumb, crumb, crumb. That's what these young guys are, crumbs. It's never going to go anywhere. You might as well get a supply of little diplomas and hats to hand out because it's like you're a training school for young men.

ANGIE: That's true, when we break up I can hand them their little diplomas and say, "Congratulations, you now have what it takes to be a good boyfriend. You can communicate, you're great in bed, you know good restaurants — and remember; IF IT ISN'T JEWELRY IT'S NOT A GIFT. You are now free to find the age-appropriate girl of your choice and make her happy."

KERRY: You know it's kinda like you went back to acting the way you did in college after Frankie died. You're not a kid anymore. You're gonna be forty soon.*

ANGIE: Shut up.

KERRY: Well it's true, and you can't go on like this. For your birthday instead of a card that says "Life Begins at Forty," I'll have to find one that says, "Forty and Still Fucking."** Why can't you just slow down and stop trying so hard to meet guys?

ANGIE: Because I hate my life. I hate my apartment. I hate the quiet. I'll do anything not to hear the fucking quiet. I went from living in a big house in Rockland to a studio apartment in Brooklyn. You think it's easy? If I start adopting cats please shoot me.

KERRY: Deal.

* or fifty soon.
** or a card that says "Fifty Is Nifty," I'll have to find one that says "Fifty and Still Fucking."

(Actresses can choose either depending on age range.)

END OF SCENE

Reflex Action
Doug Craven

Comic

Itchy and Knee, fourteen-plus, could be any sex, actually

> *In this introductory scene, Itchy and Knee, two generic characters in a self-reflexive drama, discuss their situation. Eventually, their dialogue leads to conflict . . . and a very dramatic conflict it is!*

KNEE: You know, I've noticed that most drama is just two people talking.
ITCHY: Really?
KNEE: Yes, and they generally chatter aimlessly until something happens.
ITCHY: Is that so?
KNEE: Yes.
ITCHY: Except for the occasional long pause.

> *(Long pause.)*

KNEE: Then what happens?
ITCHY: Hmm?
KNEE: After the pause.

> *(Pause.)*

> I said, "And then what happens?"

ITCHY: Oh, generally a cue.
KNEE: Like what?

> *(A phone rings.)*

ITCHY: I'll get it.
KNEE: No, don't. There's no suspense if you answer it right away.
ITCHY: Oh.

> *(It rings again.)*

KNEE: You know the funny thing about phones in theater, as opposed to real-life phones you and I enjoy and use almost daily, Itchy, is that they so rarely ring at regular intervals. *(He pauses. The phone finally rings.)* They seem to wait for the character to finish his lines. *(Long pause.)* And then they ring.

(The phone rings.)

ITCHY: I'll get it, Knee. *(Pause.)* Where do you keep your phone?

KNEE: I keep it over there. Under that Special.

ITCHY: The what?

KNEE: The blue light.

(A blue special shines down.)

ITCHY: I still don't see it.

KNEE: *(Moving to answer the phone.)* Right here. *(He answers the phone and hands the invisible receiver to Itchy.)* It's one of those mime phones.

ITCHY: Oh, I was going to buy one of those myself. Hello? Yes? Yes? Really? When? Well! *(He hangs up.)*

KNEE: You know, it's strange that you didn't give him time to answer any of your questions.

ITCHY: Yes, wasn't it? Even more strangely, I heard everything he said.

KNEE: Who was it?

ITCHY: It was my Arch-Nemesis, Professor Unfrenabulous, Master of the Dark Domain.

KNEE: How did he get my number?

ITCHY: I have "Call Forwarding."

KNEE: Ah.

ITCHY: Well, you don't want to miss an important call like that one.

KNEE: What did he say?

ITCHY: He just called to introduce The Conflict. He's planning to drop by later with his Hideous Army of the Putrefying Undead. He says that he will have some information that will be of great interest to me, and that he plans to wreak horrible revenge on me and to torment and kill us both. And then the zombies will eat our eyeballs.

KNEE: Well! What an interesting and dare I say Dramatic Premise!

ITCHY: I know. If this were a play, which it is not, but is, in fact, real life, we could now do a number of things.

KNEE: What are our options?

ITCHY: Well, we could become more and more tense as the pressure wears at us, until finally the thin veneer of Western civilization peels away, leaving us shouting at each other in a feral sort of way.

KNEE: Never happen.

ITCHY: Yes, it could.

KNEE: No.

ITCHY: I said, "yes."

KNEE: How would you know?

ITCHY: I do have a Masters degree, you know. I majored in Pinter.

KNEE: Always dragging out that damned degree, aren't you, Itchy? You know, I'm sick of hearing about it.

ITCHY: I'm sick of your resentment!

KNEE: I advance on you!

ITCHY: I respond!

KNEE: I'm sick of your superior attitude. Why don't you just cut out this shit — this SHIT! — and reveal the hidden underpinnings of our relationship?

ITCHY: All right! I will! Ever since I got drunk at that Frat Party and my boyhood sweetheart lost her virginity to another man on the same day that my father gambled away the family homestead while drunk on overproof rum, and YOU failed to assuage my wounded soul and live up to my lofty hero worship of you, I have felt . . . less than adequate.

KNEE: I had no idea. Is it too painful to discuss?

ITCHY: Very nearly. It makes me want to pause.

(Pause.)

KNEE: The man who — with your sweetheart . . . who won your family farm, was he . . . could he have been . . . Professor Unf —

ITCHY: Don't! Don't go on!

KNEE: I'm sorry. I'll comfort you during a long pause.

(He comforts him during a long pause.)

ITCHY: Thank you. That was cathartic.

KNEE: For me, too.

END OF SCENE

Tangled Web
Frederick Stroppel

Comic
Ruth and Woman, both thirties, both wearing a red dress

> *A coffee bar in N.Y.C. Ruth, a thirtyish woman in a red dress, rea-*
> *sonably attractive if a bit chunky, sits at a table, a book open be-*
> *fore her. She reads intermittently, her eyes more often watching the*
> *door. A beautiful woman, also wearing a red dress, enters from the*
> *side with a cup of coffee. She sits at a nearby table, opens a book,*
> *starts reading. Ruth watches her with dismay. She realizes something*
> *has to be said.*

RUTH: Excuse me.

WOMAN: Yes?

RUTH: Well — This is a little embarrassing, but I'm meeting someone here.

WOMAN: Really? So am I. But I guess that's not so surprising. This is the sort of place where people meet.

RUTH: Yes. The thing is, I'm meeting this guy for the first time. I don't know what he looks like, he doesn't know what I look like. So I told him I would be wearing a red dress, and reading *The DaVinci Code,* and that's how he would recognize me.

WOMAN: Yes, me too.

RUTH: Me too what?

WOMAN: I'm meeting a gentleman for the first time. I told him I'd be wearing red and reading *The DaVinci Code.*

RUTH: Oh. Well. This is rather awkward.

WOMAN: A remarkable coincidence, I would say.

RUTH: Not that it should be a problem. Because the guy — the gentle-man — I'm meeting is going to be wearing a red tie, and carrying a rose.

WOMAN: Mine too.

RUTH: Yours too? Carrying a rose? *(The Woman nods.)* This is a little hard to believe.

WOMAN: Yes, it is.

RUTH: I mean, the odds that we would both come to the same coffee bar at the same time, and we're both dressed the same, and the guys we're meeting are dressed the same.

WOMAN: Yes.

RUTH: I mean, unless we're both meeting the same guy . . . !

(They both laugh. Beat.)

RUTH: Neal?

WOMAN: *(Nods.)* Neal.

TOGETHER: *(And at the same time.)* Butterfield.

RUTH: *(Shocked.)* Oh, my God. He's a stockbroker? Lives in Englewood?

WOMAN: *(Nods.)* Drives a Lexus.

RUTH: Holy shit! Can you believe this? It has to be the same guy. Has to be.

WOMAN: So it would appear.

RUTH: What is he, crazy? He makes a date with two women for the same time? What is that all about?

WOMAN: It makes you wonder, doesn't it?

RUTH: He must have gotten his days mixed up. Maybe he thinks he's meeting me tomorrow, or next week. Oh, that's funny. He's gonna feel like such a jerk when he walks in.

WOMAN: It's certainly an amusing situation.

RUTH: *(Apprehensive.)* Unless he does want us both here at the same time, for some kind of kinky reason. Like maybe he's a serial killer, and he likes killing women in pairs? Wearing red? *(Shudders.)* Ohh, that's creepy. I don't even want to think about it.

WOMAN: *(Unconcerned.)* There are too many witnesses.

RUTH: You're right. He probably just screwed up. But how do you like that? Telling me how lonely he is, how hard it is to meet someone he can really talk to, that's why he's surfing the chat rooms . . . See, I met him on the Internet; this is one of those computer things. Big mistake, right? We've never even talked on the phone. We thought it would be more romantic that way. More romantic! Jesus.

WOMAN: I met him on the Internet, too.

RUTH: Wow. Wow! What an asshole. I should have known. Stockbrokers!

WOMAN: Yes. Well.

    (Goes back to her book.)

RUTH: This doesn't bother you?

WOMAN: Umm . . . Not really.

RUTH: The fact that he's asked us both out on the same night? Had us
    show up in the same place, wearing the same clothes, with the same
    stupid book?

WOMAN: People make mistakes.

RUTH: So you're going to stay?

WOMAN: I have no other plans.

RUTH: Neither do I, but . . . *(Shrugs.)* Maybe you're right. He's the one
    who's going to look foolish, after all. It'll be fun, watching him try
    to explain himself. Plus, I really have to get a look at this guy. This
    big fucking stud. "Neal." Sounds like somebody who collects stamps,
    doesn't it? Neal, here we are. Two gorgeous sexy women, but it's too
    late, you already blew it. Take your fancy Lexus and shove it up
    your . . . ! *(She catches herself, quiets down.)* By the way, my name is
    Ruth. *(Shakes her hand.)*

WOMAN: I'm Ruth, too.

RUTH: No! *(Woman nods her head.)* Oh, no. This gets weirder all the time.
    I don't know if I really want to meet this guy, he sounds like a psy-
    cho. But we're together, we should be able to handle him, no prob-
    lem. Solidarity, right? You know what I think we should do? We
    should really humiliate him. We should make him eat dirt. We should
    pull his pants off and pour hot coffee on his crotch . . . no, maybe
    that's too much, but we need to make a point. These stockbrokers,
    they think they own the world. Arrogant, self-centered snobs. I hate
    them.

WOMAN: Why did you agree to meet Neal, then?

RUTH: Well, you know — it's only a date.

WOMAN: But you must have felt some kind of positive connection with
    him. Didn't you think he was funny? All his jokes and clever puns?
    And what about his old-fashioned values, his sense of family? That
    must have appealed to you.

RUTH: Of course he said all the right things when he was looking for a
    date. Don't they always? Came off like a prince. Very slick with his

words. I'm sure he wrote the same bullshit to you, and God knows how many other women. Seducing as many as he could, and then trimming his list by process of elimination . . . The bastard. You can bet the only reason he's meeting me is because he thinks I'm this high-society babe. He thinks I'm an art dealer.

WOMAN: Why does he think that?

RUTH: Because that's what I told him.

WOMAN: And you're not?

RUTH: No. Well, I'm a cashier at the Metropolitan Museum of Art. Which is pretty close. I do deal in the experience of art, for which money is exchanged.

WOMAN: Interesting. As it happens, I *am* an art dealer.

RUTH: *(Amazed anew.)* This is incredible. And do you have your own gallery?

WOMAN: On West Broadway.

RUTH: That's where I said mine was! I almost said it was on Madison, but we could walk there from here, and I didn't want to put myself in an embarrassing situation. Like I should have worried.

WOMAN: So you've been lying to Neal about yourself?

RUTH: Not lying. Stretching the truth. That's just standard dating procedure. Everybody does that.

WOMAN: I don't.

RUTH: Well . . . You don't have to. You already have it all.

WOMAN: Oh, I wouldn't say that.

RUTH: Look at you. If I had your body . . . I mean, that's the funny thing — you have all the qualities I told Neal I . . .

(Ruth stops cold. She stares at the Woman a long moment.)

WOMAN: Yes?

RUTH: Who are you, anyway?

WOMAN: I told you — I'm Ruth.

RUTH: Yeah, "Ruth" — I believe that. What are you really doing here?

WOMAN: I beg your pardon?

RUTH: Who put you up to this? Is this some kind of joke? Am I being filmed?

WOMAN: Why do you ask that?

RUTH: Because this has got to be more than a coincidence! Your face, your whole look, everything about you — You're almost the way I described myself.

WOMAN: I'm exactly the way you described yourself. Exactly.

RUTH: *(Mystified.)* How do you know?

WOMAN: Because that's who I am. I'm the ideal You.

RUTH: You're the what?

WOMAN: The ideal You. The fantasy woman you created. Here I am.
(Beat.)

RUTH: I'm getting a little confused.

WOMAN: It's very simple. When you tried to sell yourself to Neal, tried to make yourself engaging and desirable, you naturally exaggerated your positive traits and minimized your negative ones. Standard dating procedure. You imagined the woman that you wanted to be, and you sent that image blithely into cyberspace, little thinking that your whimsy would take tangible form under the principles of organization that have steadily accreted in the system over the years, due to a ceaseless flow of inputted information.

RUTH: You can't be me. I would never use a word like "accreted." I don't even know what it means.

WOMAN: But your Fantasy Self does. She's as brilliant and accomplished as you are bland and uninteresting. Yes, Ruth, I've been digitally generated out of your ambitions and insecurities. I'm the realization of your deepest hopes and the defeat of your darkest fears. I'm your wish fulfilled.

RUTH: So you're a computer trick. You're not really real.

WOMAN: Ah, but computers have sufficiently blurred the distinctions between the virtually real and the really real, haven't they? So many seeds of thought and energy have been scattered willy-nilly throughout the fertile cyber-landscape that a whole teeming world has taken root. And out of that rich primordial topsoil, life springs forth. Can a computer trick drain a cup of mocha latte to its satisfying dregs? *(Woman takes one final sip, turns her cup upside down.)* Maybe, maybe not.

RUTH: I see what's going on here. This is a dream. I'm having an anxiety dream. *(The Woman pinches Ruth's arm.)* Oww!

WOMAN: No dream, sweetheart. I'm real and I'm ready.

RUTH: Ready for what?

WOMAN: Ready to meet Neal. That's why I'm here. I'm his Ruth.

RUTH: Wait a minute. Let's get something straight: I'm Ruth. And I'm meeting Neal. He's mine.

WOMAN: Oh, please. When he walks through that door, who do you think he's going to make a beeline for — you or me? Have you taken a good look at me? I'm spectacular. Built to perfection, just as you decreed. Perfect skin, perfect teeth. I even have a perfect undimpled ass, which was so considerate of you, and I'm very grateful.

RUTH: I never said a word to Neal about my ass.

WOMAN: But it was implied in the subtext. You've created the perfect match, and your satisfaction will lie in passively observing the perfect courtship. Now why don't you go into the other room and curl up with your book? I'll let you know how things go with Neal.

RUTH: No, I won't go. I worked long and hard for this date — got my hair done, waxed my legs and everything — and I'm not going to just roll over without a fight.

WOMAN: Please, Ruth, for your own sake. You're like a cousin to me, I don't want to see you humiliate yourself.

RUTH: You may be beautiful and brilliant and all that, but I'm an actual human being. That has to be an advantage.

WOMAN: Human beings are a dime a dozen; this place is crawling with them. I'm the only fantasy in town. Believe me, he's not even going to see you.

RUTH: You're awfully self-assured for someone who doesn't even have a self.

WOMAN: Hey, just because I'm computer-generated, it doesn't mean I'm one-dimensional. This is the point you're missing: I'm not shallower than you. I'm deeper. I have all of your qualities, plus a whole raft of better ones. I'm the new and improved version. You can't compete with me. You can't.

RUTH: So I'll rush back to my computer and take out the improvements. I'll give you warts, and varicose veins. I'll give you a spastic colon.

WOMAN: I don't think you have time.

END OF SCENE

Those Who Can, Do
Brighde Mullins

Dramatic
Marion, forties; Ann Marie, thirties

> *Marion is the Chair of Staten Island Community College's English department; Ann Marie is a poet. Ann Marie is being harassed by a student and she seeks help from her boss.*

ANN MARIE: I just wanted to do something meaningful.

MARION: Where did you get the notion that teaching poetry would be meaningful, Ann Marie?

ANN MARIE: Why are you here? Don't you want to lead a meaningful life?

MARION: I'm a simple woman, Ann Marie.

ANN MARIE: I'm trying to teach and under these circumstances it's been very difficult!

MARION: What circumstances are you talking about, Ann Marie?

ANN MARIE: Last week Celia brought in a large taco salad to the class. And she sat eating it loudly.

MARION: This is a state institution, Ann Marie. She'd have to open fire on the classroom to be thrown out. Last year we had a student who had a psychotic break in class. We've had students write threatening fantasies about dismembering their classmates. They're *expressing* themselves. It's freedom of speech. These students know their rights to an education. There's not a lot that you can do.

ANN MARIE: But I can't really do a good job under these circumstances.

MARION: *(Brightly.)* Then why don't you just do a bad job?

ANN MARIE: Are you seriously telling me to do a bad job?

Are you serious?

MARION: Listen, Ann Marie, you're not the only one who's had problems with Celia.

(Long beat: she looks through a manila file folder.)

She has taken several Creative Writing classes. It looks like she's in her seventeenth year here.

ANN MARIE: But how could she remain in school that long? Isn't there a statute of limitations on attending college? She clearly cannot function.

MARION: Maybe she was taking her meds in the past.

ANN MARIE: Her meds?

MARION: Medications.

ANN MARIE: What kind of medications?

MARION: I'm not at liberty to disclose the facts of her file.

But I can give you some general info: She started taking classes in 1984, about the time that Reagan emptied out the psychiatric wards around the city. That's your first clue. A lot of those folks got advised to explore their creativity as a way to control their delusions, et cetera. If you ask me I would have to say that Ronald Reagan did those folks a disservice.

ANN MARIE: You won't find me defending Ronald Reagan. What else does it say?

MARION: *(Smiling.)* I'm really not at liberty to say.

ANN MARIE: Don't I have a right to know who it is that I'm dealing with?

MARION: She's protected by the privacy of information act.

ANN MARIE: Am I protected?

MARION: You have to go through the proper channels.

ANN MARIE: Which are what?

MARION: Well, we do have a campus police department. You might try calling them.

ANN MARIE: OK. I will.

MARION: You might think of Teaching as some meaningful occupation because you had this Joycean epiphany on the IRT, but for most of us, it's a job. It's a public service job. The Great State of New York cuts your paycheck. You are essentially a civil servant and we are educating these kids not for the Heights of Parnassus, not for the cafes of Greenwich Village, not for salon society, we are educating them to be data processors and shift managers at Strawberry's, capesce?

(Beat.)

We need Celia's tuition. We need her body in that chair.

We are providing a public service.

END OF SCENE